SAT®
Reading &
Writing Prep

RELATED TITLES

8 Practice Tests for the SAT

SAT Math Prep

PSAT Prep with 2 Practice Tests

SAT Total Prep

SAT Prep Plus with 5 Practice Tests

SAT Prep with 2 Practice Tests

SAT®
Reading &
Writing Prep

Acknowledgments

Special thanks to those who made this book possible including Arthur Ahn, Laura Aitcheson, Becky Berthiaume, Michael Boothroyd, Matthew Callan, Potoula Chresomales, Dom Eggert, Kate Fisher, Katy Haynicz-Smith, Adam Hinz, Kate Hurley, Brandon Jones, Rebecca Knauer, Celina Lasota, Terrence McMullen, James Radkins, Justin Starr, Bob Verini, Lee Weiss, Devon Wible, Daniel Wittich, and many others who contributed materials and advice.

SAT® is a trademark registered and/or owned by the College Board, which was not involved in the production of, and does not endorse, this product.

This publication is designed to provide accurate and authoritative information in regard to the subject matter covered. It is sold with the understanding that the publisher is not engaged in rendering legal, accounting, or other professional service. If legal advice or other expert assistance is required, the services of a competent professional should be sought.

Kaplan Publishing books are available at special quantity discounts to use for sales promotions, employee premiums, or educational purposes. For more information or to purchase books, please call the Simon & Schuster Special Sales Department at 866-506-1949.

Table of Contents

SECTION ONE: THE READING TEST

SECTION TWO: THE WRITING & LANGUAGE TEST

SECTION THREE: THE ESSAY TEST

SECTION FOUR: PRACTICE TEST

How to Use This Book

BECOME FAMILIAR WITH THE SAT EVIDENCE-BASED READING AND WRITING AND ESSAY TESTS

Learn the structure of the SAT Reading, Writing, and Essay Tests—what kinds of questions appear on them, how they are scored, and how to best approach each one. Knowing what to expect will set you up for success as you prepare. You will find all the information you need in the next few pages of Kaplan's SAT Reading & Writing Prep.

PRACTICE SETS

This book contains a total of 19 practice sets: eight for Reading, eight for Writing & Language, and three for the Essay. Each section is preceded by a brief instructional review that includes the applicable Kaplan Methods and Strategies for that part of the SAT.

ANSWERS & EXPLANATIONS

Following each practice set, you will find detailed answers and explanations. Use these to determine why you answered a question incorrectly and how to avoid the same mistakes on similar questions in the future. Each explanation includes both advice on how to approach similar questions and a detailed step-by-step solution. Read the explanations for questions you answered correctly to ensure your reasoning in selecting the correct answer was sound.

PRACTICE TEST

When you have completed all of the practice sets, take the Practice Test under test-like conditions, using the timing indicated for each section of the test, which is approximately two-and-a-half hours long. Make sure to check your answers, calculate your score using the conversion chart provided, and read the answers and explanations to reinforce what you've learned.

Introduction to SAT Evidence-Based Reading and Writing

The Evidence-Based Reading and Writing section of the redesigned SAT is broken down into two sections: the Reading Test and the Writing & Language Test. Your scores from each of these two tests will range from 10 to 40. These scores will be summed and then scaled to a 200–800 score.

THE READING TEST

The SAT Reading Test will focus on your comprehension and reasoning skills when presented with challenging extended prose passages taken from a variety of content areas.

SAT Reading Test Overview	
Timing	65 minutes
Questions	52 passage-based multiple-choice questions
Passages	4 single passages; 1 set of paired passages
Passage Length	500–750 words per passage or passage set

Passages will draw from U.S. and World Literature, History/Social Studies, and Science. One set of History/Social Studies or Science passages will be paired. History/Social Studies and Science passages can also be accompanied by graphical representations of data such as charts, graphs, tables, and so on.

Reading Test Passage Types	
U.S. and World Literature	1 passage with 10 questions
History/Social Studies	2 passages or 1 passage and 1 paired passage set with 10–11 questions each
Science	2 passages or 1 passage and 1 paired passage set with 10–11 questions each

The multiple-choice questions for each passage will be arranged in order from the more general to the more specific so that you can actively engage with the entire passage before answering questions about details.

Skills Tested by Reading Test Questions	
Information and Ideas	Close reading, citing textual evidence, determining central ideas and themes
Summarizing	Understanding relationships, interpreting words and phrases in context
Rhetoric	Analyzing word choice, assessing overall text structure, assessing part-whole relationships, analyzing point of view, determining purpose, analyzing arguments
Synthesis	Analyzing multiple texts, analyzing quantitative information

THE WRITING & LANGUAGE TEST

The SAT Writing & Language Test will focus on your ability to revise and edit text from a range of content areas.

SAT Writing & Language Test Overview	
Timing	35 minutes
Questions	44 passage-based multiple-choice questions
Passages	4 single passages
Passage Length	400–450 words per passage

The SAT Writing & Language Test will contain four single passages, one from each of the following subject areas: Careers, Humanities, History/Social Studies, and Science.

Writing & Language Test Passage Types	
Careers	Hot topics in "major fields of work" such as information technology and health care
Humanities	Texts about literature, art, history, music, and philosophy pertaining to human culture
History/Social Studies	Discussion of historical or social sciences topics such as anthropology, communication studies, economics, education, human geography, law, linguistics, political science, psychology, and sociology
Science	Exploration of concepts, findings, and discoveries in the natural sciences including Earth science, biology, chemistry, and physics

Some passages and/or questions will refer to one or more informational graphic(s) that represent(s) data. Questions associated with these graphical representations will ask you to revise and edit the passage based on the data presented in the graphic.

The most prevalent question format on the SAT Writing & Language Test will ask you to choose the best of three alternatives to an underlined portion of the passage or to decide that the current version is the best option. You will be asked to improve the development, organization, and diction in the passages to ensure they conform to conventional standards of English grammar, usage, and style.

Skills Tested by Writing & Language Test Questions	
Expression of Ideas (24 questions)	Development, organization, and effective language use
Standard English Conventions (20 questions)	Sentence structure, conventions of usage, and conventions of punctuation

Introduction to the SAT Essay Test

The SAT Essay Test is optional. Its aim is to assess your college and career readiness by testing your abilities to read and analyze a high-quality source document and write a coherent analysis of the source supported with critical reasoning and evidence from the given text.

The SAT Essay Test features an argumentative source text of 650–750 words aimed toward a large audience. Passages will examine ideas, debates, and shifts in the arts and sciences as well as civic, cultural, and political life. Rather than having a simple for/against structure, these passages will be nuanced and will relate views on complex subjects. These passages will also be logical in their structure and reasoning.

It is important to note that prior knowledge is not required.

The SAT Essay Test prompt will ask you to explain how the presented passage's author builds an argument to convince an audience. In writing your essay, you may analyze elements such as the author's use of evidence, reasoning, style, and persuasion; you will not be limited to those elements listed, however. Rather than writing about whether you agree or disagree with the presented argument, you will write an essay in which you analyze how the author makes an argument.

The SAT Essay Test will be broken down into three categories for scoring: Reading, Analysis, and Writing. Each of these elements will be scored on a scale of 1 to 4 by two graders, for a total score of 2 to 8 for each category.

Test-Taking Strategies

The SAT is different from the tests you are used to taking in school. The good news is that you can use the SAT's particular structure to your advantage.

For example, on a test given in school, you probably go through the questions in order. You spend more time on the harder questions than on the easier ones because harder questions are usually worth more points. You probably often show your work because your teacher tells you that how you approach a question is as important as getting the correct answer.

This approach is not optimal for the SAT. On the SAT, you benefit from moving around within a section if you come across tough questions because the harder questions are worth the same number of points as the easier questions. It doesn't matter how you arrive at the correct answer—only that you bubble in the correct answer choice.

STRATEGY #1: TRIAGING THE TEST

You do not need to complete questions on the SAT in order. Every student has different strengths and should attack the test with those strengths in mind. Your main objective on the SAT should be to score as many points as you can. While approaching questions out of order may seem counterintuitive, it is a surefire way to achieve your best score.

Just remember, you can skip around within each section, but you cannot work on a section other than the one you've been instructed to work on.

- First, work through all the easy questions that you can do quickly. Skip questions that are hard or time-consuming

- For the Reading and Writing & Language Tests, start with the passage you find most manageable and work toward the one you find most challenging. You do not need to go in order

- Second, work through the questions that are doable but time-consuming

- Third, work through the hard questions

- If you run out of time, pick a Letter of the Day for remaining questions

A Letter of the Day is an answer choice letter (A, B, C, or D) that you choose before Test Day to select for questions you guess on.

STRATEGY #2: ELIMINATION

Even though there is no wrong-answer penalty on the SAT, Elimination is still a crucial strategy. If you can determine that one or more answer choices are definitely incorrect, you can increase your chances of getting the right answer by paring the selection down.

To eliminate answer choices, do the following:

- Read each answer choice

- Cross out the answer choices that are incorrect

- Remember: There is no wrong-answer penalty, so take your best guess

STRATEGY #3: GUESSING

Each multiple-choice question on the SAT has four answer choices and no wrong-answer penalty. That means if you have no idea how to approach a question, you have a 25 percent chance of randomly choosing the correct answer. Even though there's a 75 percent chance of selecting the incorrect answer, you won't lose any points for doing so. The worst that can happen on the SAT is that you'll earn zero points on a question, which means you should always at least take a guess, even when you have no idea what to do.

When guessing on a question, do the following:

- Always try to strategically eliminate answer choices before guessing

- If you run out of time, or have no idea what a question is asking, pick a Letter of the Day

Common Testing Myths

Since its inception, the SAT has gone through various revisions, but it has always been an integral part of the college admissions process. As a result of its significance and the changes it has undergone, a number of rumors and myths have circulated about the exam. In this section, we'll dispel some of the most common ones. As always, you can find the most up-to-date information about the SAT at the CollegeBoard website (www.collegeboard.org).

Myth: **There is a wrong-answer penalty on the SAT to discourage guessing.**

Fact: While this statement was true a few years ago, it is no longer true. Older versions of the SAT had a wrong-answer penalty so that students who guessed on questions would not have an advantage over students who left questions blank. This penalty has been removed; make sure you never leave an SAT question blank!

Myth: **Answer choice C is most likely to be the correct answer.**

Fact: This rumor has roots in human psychology. Apparently, when people such as high school teachers, for example, design an exam, they have a slight bias toward answer choice C when assigning correct answers. While humans do write SAT questions, a computer randomizes the distribution of correct choices; statistically, therefore, each answer choice is equally likely to be the correct answer.

Myth: **The SAT is just like another test in school.**

Fact: While the SAT covers some of the same content as your high school literature and English classes, it also presents concepts in ways that are fundamentally different. The SAT places a heavy emphasis on working through questions as quickly and efficiently as possible.

Myth: **You have to get all the questions right to get a perfect score.**

Fact: Many students have reported missing several questions on the SAT and being pleasantly surprised to receive perfect scores. Their experience is not atypical: Usually, you can miss a few questions and still get a coveted perfect score. The makers of the SAT use a technique called scaling to ensure that a SAT score conveys the same information from year to year, so you might be able to miss a couple more questions on a slightly harder SAT exam and miss fewer questions on an easier SAT exam and get the same scores. Keep a positive attitude throughout the SAT, and in many cases, your scores will pleasantly surprise you.

Myth: **You can't prepare for the SAT.**

Fact: You've already proven this myth false by buying this book. While the SAT is designed to fairly test students regardless of preparation, you can gain a huge advantage by familiarizing yourself with the structure and content of the exam. By working through the questions and practice tests available to you, you'll ensure that nothing on the SAT catches you by surprise and that you do everything you can to maximize your score. Your Kaplan resources help you structure this practice in the most efficient way possible, and provide you with helpful strategies and tips as well.

The Reading Test

The Kaplan Method for Reading Comprehension

Use the Kaplan Method for Reading Comprehension to analyze every SAT Reading passage and question you encounter, whether practicing, completing your homework, working on a Practice Test, or taking the actual exam on Test Day.

The Kaplan Method for Reading Comprehension consists of three steps:

Step 1: Read actively

Step 2: Examine the question stem

Step 3: Predict and answer

Step 1: Read actively

Active reading means:

- Ask questions and take notes as you read the passage. Asking questions about the passage and taking notes is an integral part of your approach to acing the SAT Reading Test.

Some of the questions you might want to ask are:

- Why did the author write this word/detail/sentence/paragraph?
- Is the author taking a side? If so, what side is he or she taking?
- What are the tone and purpose of the passage?

Make sure you remember to:

- Identify the passage type.
- Take notes, circle keywords, and underline key phrases. All of these notes and markings are called a "Passage Map."

Step 2: Examine the question stem

This means you should:

- Identify keywords and line references in the question stem.
- Apply question-type strategies as necessary

Step 3: Predict and answer

This means you should:

- Predict an answer before looking at the answer choices, also known as "predict before you peek."
- Select the best match.

Predicting before you peek helps you:

- Eliminate the possibility of falling into wrong answer traps.

Passage Mapping

Step 1 of the Kaplan Method for Reading Comprehension dictates that you must take notes as you read the passage. These notes are called a Passage Map because they guide you through the passage and will lead you to the correct answers.

Make sure you pay attention and make note of the following when you map the passage:

- The "why" or the central idea of the passage—in other words, the thesis statement
- Transitions or changes in direction in a passage's logic
- The author's opinions and other opinions the author cites
- The author's tone and purpose

While Passage Mapping may seem time-consuming at first, it will be second nature by Test Day, and your overall Reading Test timing will greatly improve because you'll be spending less time searching the passage for answers to the questions.

SAT experts always map Reading Test passages. Look at the test-like excerpt that follows. Make sure you spend some time looking over the sample Passage Map—these are the types of notes you should practice taking as you read Reading Test passages.

The following passage details how scientists use radioisotopes to date artifacts and remains.

Archaeologists often rely on measuring the amounts of different atoms present in an item from a site to determine its age. The identity of an atom depends on how many protons it has in its nucleus; for example, all carbon atoms have 6 protons. Each atom of an element, however, can have a different number of neutrons, so there can be several versions, or isotopes, of each element. Scientists name the isotopes by the total number of protons plus neutrons. For example, a carbon atom with 6 neutrons is carbon-12 while a carbon atom with 7 neutrons is carbon-13.

Some combinations of protons and neutrons are not stable and will change over time. For example, carbon-14, which has 6 protons and 8 neutrons, will slowly change into nitrogen-14, with 7 protons and 7 neutrons. Scientists can directly measure the amount of carbon-12 and carbon-14 in a sample or they can use radiation measurements to calculate these amounts. Each atom of carbon-14 that changes to nitrogen-14 emits radiation. Scientists can measure the rate of emission and use that to calculate the total amount of carbon-14 present in a sample.

Carbon-14 atoms are formed in the atmosphere at the same rate at which they decay. Therefore, the ratio of carbon-12 to carbon-14 atoms in the atmosphere is constant. Living plants and animals have the same ratio of carbon-12 to carbon-14 in their tissues because they are constantly taking in carbon in the form of food or carbon dioxide. After the plant or animal dies, however, it stops taking in carbon and so the amount of carbon-14 atoms in its tissues starts to decrease at a predictable rate.

By measuring the ratio of carbon-12 to carbon-14 in a bone, for example, a scientist can determine how long the animal the bone came from has been dead. To determine an object's age this way is called "carbon-14 dating." Carbon-14 dating can be performed on any material made by a living organism, such as wood or paper from trees or bones and skin from animals. Materials with ages up to about 50,000 years old can be dated. By finding the age of several objects found at different depths at an archeological dig, the archeologists can then make a timeline for the layers of the site. Objects in the same layer will be about the same age. By using carbon dating for a few objects in a layer, archeologists know the age of other objects in that layer, even if the layer itself cannot be carbon dated.

definition of isotope & examples

all atoms of one element have same # protons, diff. # neutrons

isotopes unstable; measure carb-14

carb-14 tom decay predictable

how carb-14 dating is used → timelines based on layers

The Kaplan Method for Infographics

Both the SAT Reading Test and the SAT Writing & Language Test will contain one or more passages and/or questions that include one or more infographics. Each infographic will convey or expand on information from or related to the passage.

The Kaplan Method for Infographics consists of three steps:

Step 1: Read the question

Step 2: Examine the infographic

Step 3: Predict and answer

Step 1: Read the question

Assess the question stem for information that will help you zero-in on the specific parts of the infographic that apply to the question.

Step 2: Examine the infographic

Make sure to:

- Circle parts of the infographic that relate directly to the question
- Identify units of measurement, labels, and titles

Step 3: Predict and answer

Just as in Step 3 of the Kaplan Method for Reading Comprehension, do not look at the answer choices until you've used the infographic to make a prediction.

Kaplan's Top Points for SAT Reading

COMMAND OF EVIDENCE QUESTIONS

A Command of Evidence question relies on your answer to the question that precedes it. These questions require you to identify the portion of the text that provides the best evidence for the conclusion you reached when selecting your answer to the previous question.

Kaplan's Strategy for Command of Evidence questions involves retracing your steps; that is, you must return to the previous question to ensure you answer the Command of Evidence question correctly. The question preceding a Command of Evidence question can be any other question type.

To answer Command of Evidence questions efficiently and correctly, employ the following Kaplan Strategy:

- When you see a question asking you to choose the best evidence to support your answer to the previous question, review how you selected that answer

- Avoid answers that provide evidence for incorrect answers to the previous question

- The correct answer will support why the previous question's answer is correct

Command of Evidence questions ask that you cite the textual evidence that best supports a given claim or point. The given claim or point will be the correct answer choice to the previous question. Then, you will choose one of the four excerpts from the passage as the best evidence or support for that answer.

The first step to approaching a Command of Evidence question is to make sure you answered the previous question—no matter its type—correctly. If you answer the question preceding a Command of Evidence question incorrectly, you have a smaller chance of selecting the correct answer.

VOCAB-IN-CONTEXT QUESTIONS

Vocab-in-Context questions require you to deduce the meaning of a word or phrase by using the context in which the word or phrase appears. You can recognize Vocab-in-Context questions because the wording of the question stem is often like this: "As used in line 7, 'clairvoyant' most nearly means …"

Kaplan's Strategy for Vocab-in-Context questions relies heavily on Step 3 of the Kaplan Method for Reading Comprehension: Predict and answer.

To answer Vocab-in-Context questions efficiently and correctly, employ the following Kaplan Strategy:

- Pretend the word is a blank in the sentence
- Predict what word could be substituted for the blank
- Select the answer choice that best matches your prediction

GLOBAL QUESTIONS

Global questions require you to both identify explicit and determine implicit central ideas or themes in a text. If you pay attention to the big picture—the author's central idea and purpose—while reading SAT Reading passages, you will be able to answer Global questions with little to no rereading of the passage. To fully understand the central ideas and themes of a passage, you must synthesize the different points the author makes with his or her thesis statement, which you should underline when Passage Mapping.

Global questions may also ask you to choose a correct summary of the passage as a whole or key information and ideas within the passage. When presented with this type of Global question, you can use your Passage Map, which is essentially a brief summary of what you have read.

You can recognize Global questions because they typically do not reference line numbers or even individual paragraphs. To confidently answer Global questions, you need to not only identify the central idea or theme of the passage but also avoid choosing answers that summarize secondary or supplementary points.

Do note there is a slight difference between nonfiction and fiction passages. Science and History/Social Studies passages are nonfiction and will have a definite central idea and thesis statement; U.S. and World Literature passages are fiction and will have a central theme but no thesis statement.

DETAIL QUESTIONS

Detail questions ask about a specific part of the passage. Because your Passage Map should note only the location of key details rather than the details themselves, you will have to refer to the passage to answer these questions.

You can recognize Detail questions because they normally include line references or phrasing that directs you to a particular part of the passage.

When answering Detail questions:

- Read around the cited text to understand the context.
- Predict by rephrasing the relevant section in your own words.
- Eliminate any answer choices that do not match your prediction.

Also, make sure to read answer choices carefully. Watch out for negatives such as *not* and *no* that change an otherwise correct answer choice into the opposite of what you are looking for.

RHETORIC QUESTIONS

Some Rhetoric questions ask about the purpose of the passage as a whole or a part of the passage. Every author has a reason for writing and including certain paragraphs, sentences, words, or details. To identify that reason—or purpose—ask these questions:

- Why did the author write this passage?
- What does the author want the reader to think about this topic?
- What is the function of this section?
- How does this section help achieve the author's purpose?

Other Rhetoric questions ask you to establish the author's perspective and how that perspective affects the content and the style of the passage. That is, you need to figure out not only what the author says but also how the author says it.

When answering these types of questions, ask:

- Is the author's tone positive, negative, or neutral?
- Does the author want things to change or stay the same?
- Is the author addressing supporters or opponents?

Some questions will ask about how a particular word or phrase affects your understanding of the author's purpose and point of view. These questions ask about the function of a word or phrase within the passage. That is, why did the author use this word or phrase?

Some Rhetoric questions will require you to analyze the structure of the passage. These questions tend to focus on the passage's form rather than its content. There are two kinds of text structures you will need to recognize on the SAT Reading Test:

1. Overall text structure refers to how the information within a passage is organized. Some common text structures are cause-and-effect, compare-and-contrast, sequence, problem-and-solution, and description.

2. Part-whole structures describe how a particular part of the passage (e.g., a sentence, quotation, or paragraph) relates to the overall text. When asked about a part-whole relationship, make sure you determine what function the part plays in the passage.

Other Rhetoric questions on the SAT Reading Test will ask you to analyze arguments within the text for both their form and content. Questions that ask you to analyze a text's arguments vary in scope. You may be asked to analyze claims and counterclaims, assess the author's reasoning, or analyze evidence presented in the passage.

READING PRACTICE SET 1

Questions 1-11 are based on the following passage.

In this excerpt, a Nobel Prize-winning scientist discusses ways of thinking about extremely long periods of time.

There is one fact about the origin of life that is reasonably certain. Whenever and wherever it happened, it started a very long time ago, so long
Line ago that it is extremely difficult to form any realistic
5 idea of such vast stretches of time. The shortness of human life necessarily limits the span of direct personal recollection.

Human culture has given us the illusion that our memories go further back than that. Before writing
10 was invented, the experience of earlier generations, embodied in stories, myths and moral precepts to guide behavior, was passed down verbally or, to a lesser extent, in pictures, carvings, and statues. Writing has made more precise and more extensive
15 the transmission of such information and, in recent times, photography has sharpened our images of the immediate past. Even so, we have difficulty in contemplating steadily the march of history, from the beginnings of civilization to the present day, in
20 such a way that we can truly experience the slow passage of time. Our minds are not built to deal comfortably with periods as long as hundreds or thousands of years.

Yet when we come to consider the origin of life,
25 the time scales we must deal with make the whole span of human history seem but the blink of an eyelid. There is no simple way to adjust one's thinking to such vast stretches of time. The immensity of time passed is beyond our ready comprehension.
30 One can only construct an impression of it from indirect and incomplete descriptions, just as a blind man laboriously builds up, by touch and sound, a picture of his immediate surroundings.

The customary way to provide a convenient
35 framework for one's thoughts is to compare the age of the universe with the length of a single Earthly day. Perhaps a better comparison, along the same lines, would be to equate the age of our earth with a single week. On such a scale the age of the universe,
40 since the Big Bang, would be about two or three weeks. The oldest macroscopic fossils (those from the start of the Cambrian period*) would have been alive just one day ago. Modern man would have appeared in the last ten seconds and agriculture in
45 the last one or two. Odysseus** would have lived only half a second before the present time.

Even this comparison hardly makes the longer time scale comprehensible to us. An alternative is to draw a linear map of time, with the different events
50 marked on it. The problem here is to make the line long enough to show our own experience on a reasonable scale, and yet short enough for convenient reproduction and examination. But perhaps the most vivid method is to compare time to the lines of print
55 themselves. Let us make a 200-page book equal in length to the time from the start of the Cambrian to the present; that is, about 600 million years. Then each full page will represent roughly 3 million years, each line about ninety thousand years and each letter
60 or small space about fifteen hundred years. The origin of the Earth would be about seven books ago and the origin of the universe (which has been dated only approximately) ten or so books before that. Almost the whole of recorded human history would be
65 covered by the last two or three letters of the book.

If you now turn back the pages of the book, slowly reading one letter at a time—remember, each letter is fifteen hundred years—then this may convey to you something of the immense stretches
70 of time we shall have to consider. On this scale the span of your own life would be less than the width of a comma.

* *Cambrian period*: the earliest period in the Paleozoic era, beginning about 600 million years ago

** *Odysseus*: the most famous Greek hero of antiquity; he is the hero of Homer's The Odyssey, which describes the aftermath of the Trojan War (ca. 1200 B.C.)

1. The central idea of the passage is that

    A) human life is short in comparison to the age of the Earth.

    B) life on the Earth started an extremely long time ago.

    C) scientists have difficulty figuring out when life began.

    D) it is hard to form a realistic sense of the vastness of time.

2. The author's stance can best be described as that of

    A) a humorist trying to make a scientific topic entertaining for readers.

    B) a scholar providing evidence to support a newly devised theory.

    C) a journalist trying to persuade readers to improve their understanding of history.

    D) an expert presenting an abstract idea in an accessible manner.

3. The passage most strongly suggests that which of the following is true of humans?

    A) A human life is extremely short relative to the span of time since the Earth began.

    B) Photography has helped humans understand the passage of time.

    C) Human development can be traced through written stories and myths, as well as artwork, of long ago.

    D) Humans have a better understanding of the age of the universe when it is compared to the length of a single day.

4. Which choice provides the best evidence for the answer to the previous question?

    A) Lines 9-12 ("Before writing ... verbally")

    B) Lines 14-17 ("Writing has made ... immediate past")

    C) Lines 34-37 ("The customary ... Earthly day")

    D) Lines 70-72 ("On this scale ... a comma")

5. The author discusses several kinds of time scales primarily to demonstrate the

    A) difficulty of assigning precise dates to past events.

    B) different choices scientists have when investigating the origin of life.

    C) evolution of efforts to comprehend the passage of history.

    D) immensity of time since life on Earth began.

6. As used in line 11, "embodied" most nearly means

    A) symbolized.

    B) exemplified.

    C) personified.

    D) embraced.

7. The author uses the analogy of the blind man in lines 31-33 to primarily show that

    A) humans are unable to comprehend long periods of time.

    B) human history occupies only a fraction of the time since life began.

    C) long periods of time can be understood only indirectly.

    D) humans refuse to learn from lessons of the past.

8. Which choice provides the best evidence for the answer to the previous question?

   A) Lines 5-7 ("The shortness … recollection")

   B) Lines 24-27 ("Yet … an eyelid")

   C) Lines 30-31 ("One can only … descriptions")

   D) Lines 63-65 ("Almost the whole … book")

9. As used in line 29, "ready" most nearly means

   A) immediate.

   B) willing.

   C) set.

   D) prepared.

10. The purpose of the references to the Big Bang and the Cambrian period in lines 39-43 is to

    A) suggest that agriculture was a relatively late development in human history.

    B) illustrate that the Earth's age can be understood using the time scale of a week.

    C) argue that there are no existing fossils that predate the Cambrian period.

    D) indicate that the Cambrian period lasted 600 million years.

11. According to lines 48-53, one difficulty in using a linear representation of time is that

    A) linear representations of time do not meet accepted scientific standards of accuracy.

    B) prehistoric eras overlap each other, making linear representation deceptive.

    C) a scale that allots enough space to show human experience clearly would make the map too long to copy and use.

    D) our knowledge of pre-Cambrian time is insufficient to construct an accurate linear map.

ANSWERS & EXPLANATIONS

1. D

2. D

3. A

4. D

5. D

6. B

7. C

8. C

9. A

10. B

11. C

1. D
Difficulty: Medium

Category: Reading / Global

Strategic Advice: Review your Passage Map notes pertaining to the entire passage to determine the author's central idea.

Getting to the Answer: While other answer choices might be implied by the passage, only (D) expresses the passage's central idea. Choices A and C are incorrect because the passage's central idea is about neither the brevity of human life nor scientists, respectively. Choice B is incorrect because only part of the passage discusses life on Earth.

2. D
Difficulty: Medium

Category: Reading / Rhetoric

Strategic Advice: An "author's stance" refers to the author's point of view or attitude toward his or her topic.

Getting to the Answer: The italicized blurb will help you correctly answer this question because it offers that the author is a Nobel Prize-winning scientist. While the ability to understand long periods of time is an abstract topic, the author discusses the subject in a way that readers can understand. Watch out for B—while the author is a scholar, there is nothing in the passage that supports that this is a newly devised theory. Choice (D) is correct.

3. A
Difficulty: Medium

Category: Reading / Inference

Strategic Advice: On the SAT, an inference is a conclusion drawn from facts in the passage. Although the correct answer will not be explicitly stated in a passage, it won't be too far removed from the author's topic and point of view.

Getting to the Answer: Throughout the passage, the author implies that human life is extremely short compared to the length of Earth's existence. In the first paragraph, the author writes that the "shortness of human life" (lines 5-6) makes it "extremely difficult to form any realistic idea" (lines 4-5) of the vastness of the existence of life on Earth. The author later adds, "Our minds are not built to deal comfortably with periods as long as hundreds or thousands of years" (lines 21-23) and that "the time scales we must deal with make the whole span of human history seem but the blink of an eyelid" (lines 25-27). Therefore, (A) is correct.

4. D
Difficulty: Medium

Category: Reading / Command of Evidence

Strategic Advice: Use your work on answering the previous question to correctly answer a Command of Evidence question. If you cannot find support for your previous answer among the answer choices to a Command of Evidence question, you should reevaluate your approach to answering the preceding question.

Getting to the Answer: Choice (D) directly supports the idea that a human life is extremely short relative to the span of time since the Earth began.

5. D

Difficulty: Hard

Category: Reading / Rhetoric

Strategic Advice: Make sure the answer choice you select fits the central idea of the passage. Most of this passage is about the vastness of time, so the correct answer will likely support this idea as well.

Getting to the Answer: Choice (D) is correct. The author describes several time scales to show how challenging it is to depict time, thus underscoring its immensity.

6. B

Difficulty: Medium

Category: Reading / Vocab-in-Context

Strategic Advice: Predict a word to replace the word cited in the question stem. Select the answer choice that best matches your prediction.

Getting to the Answer: The "experiences of earlier generations" (line 10) are not symbolized, personified, nor embraced in "stories, myths and moral precepts" (line 11). They are represented, or "exemplified;" therefore, (B) is correct.

7. C

Difficulty: Medium

Category: Reading / Inference

Strategic Advice: Determine how the author's analogy of a blind man supports the central purpose and claim of the passage.

Getting to the Answer: The analogy of a blind man who constructs a picture of his surroundings based on touch and sound helps illustrate how humans construct their understanding of the immensity of time. While a blind man indirectly gathers clues about the world around him through touch and sound, humans indirectly gather clues about the vastness of time through smaller comparisons. Choice (C) is correct.

8. C

Difficulty: Easy

Category: Reading / Command of Evidence

Strategic Advice: Review how you chose the answer to the previous question to help you determine which quotation is the best evidence.

Getting to the Answer: Choice (C) is correct because it sets up the analogy in question by depicting how humans can only indirectly construct incomplete impressions of vastness of time.

9. A

Difficulty: Medium

Category: Reading / Vocab-in-Context

Strategic Advice: Eliminate answer choices that are common definitions for "ready" but do not make sense in the context of the passage.

Getting to the Answer: In the cited line, "ready" is used as an adjective modifier of "comprehension." One primary definition of "ready" is "prepared," so eliminate D. "Ready" is also often paired with "willing" and "set," so eliminate B and C. Choice (A) is correct.

10. B

Difficulty: Medium

Category: Reading / Rhetoric

Strategic Advice: Eliminate answer choices that deal only with the Cambrian period because the question stem mentions the Big Bang as well as the Cambrian period.

Getting to the Answer: The author refers to the Big Bang and the Cambrian period to depict that the Earth's age can be understood using the time scale of a few weeks. Therefore, (B) is correct.

11. C

Difficulty: Easy

Category: Reading / Detail

Strategic Advice: Select the answer choice that matches what is explicitly stated in the cited lines.

Getting to the Answer: The passage states that the difficulty "is to make the line long enough to show our own experience on a reasonable scale, and yet short enough for convenient reproduction and examination" (lines 50-53). Choice (C) matches this summary and is correct.

READING PRACTICE SET 2

Questions 1-11 are based on the following passage and supplementary material.

The following passage details the causes and effects of Black Monday, a major global economic crisis.

On October 19, 1987, the United States stock market made a precipitous plummet, losing 22.6 percent of its value in just a single trading
Line session. Daily gains and losses are normal in stock
5 markets, but only in small amounts—usually less than 1 percent per day. But on October 19, 1987, the Dow Jones Industrial Average (DJIA) finished down 508 points, the largest one-day loss in history. The day became known as Black Monday.
10 Black Monday was the first event of its kind in a modernized, global financial industry that was considered to be immune to such catastrophes— catastrophes like the stock market crash of 1929, which started the Great Depression.
15 What caused this financial collapse in 1987? Ironically, the sophistication of the market and the advancement of a global economy were partially responsible for the instability. The world's financial markets had become "globalized," meaning that
20 companies and investors made purchases and sales in each other's markets around the world. In the months preceding the crash, foreign investors had been buying stock in the United States markets. The DJIA had gained 44 percent in just seven months.
25 While growth is healthy and profitable in stock markets, savvy traders know that rapid growth can be dangerous.
In the days before the crash, there were, in fact, portentous signs akin to crumbling rocks
30 that signaled an impending avalanche. First, on October 14th, several world markets incurred large daily losses. Second, on October 16th, many more sell-offs occurred. Third, regular expiration dates of options and futures happened to fall on this day as
35 well. The concurrence of these three events is called

"triple witching," perhaps because it's just that scary to bankers.

All weekend prior to the Monday-morning crash, Asian markets plunged. Digital communica-
40 tion was not quite as instantaneous as it is today, but traders were able to follow reports on televi- sion. United States government officials made announcements that they were prepared to respond with measures to bring stability to the value of the
45 United States dollar. Global investors liquidated their positions*, and the number of sell orders vastly outnumbered willing buyers near previous prices, creating a cascade in stock markets. In New Zealand, the stock market fell 60 percent.
50 When the opening bell rang in New York City on Monday morning, traders raced each other to the pits to sell. People said later that the sense of panic was like someone had yelled "Fire!" in a crowded room.
55 Black Monday demonstrated the unprecedented extent to which worldwide financial markets had become intertwined. Investors watched on live television as a financial crisis spread from market to market like a virus moving through a human
60 population or a computer network.
Stock markets recovered a majority of their Black Monday losses: In just two trading sessions, the DJIA gained back 288 points, or 57 percent, of the total Black Monday downturn. Fewer than two
65 years later, United States stock markets had already surpassed their pre-crash highs.
Nevertheless, a number of regulations were put in place to prevent such a crash from happening again. For example, after Black Monday, regula-
70 tors overhauled trade-clearing protocols to bring uniformity to all prominent market products. Also, a new system called a "circuit breaker" was estab- lished. This system functions like a circuit breaker

position: a market commitment in securities or commodities, or the inventory of a market trader

in an electrical grid, which is designed to stop the
75 flow of current if it becomes dangerously high. If a
large sell-off occurs in the stock market, securities
exchanges can temporarily halt trading in instances
of exceptionally large price declines. For example,
the New York Stock Exchange can temporarily halt
80 trading when the S&P 500 stock index abruptly
declines to provide investors "the ability to make
informed choices during periods of high market
volatility."

Weekly DJIA: October 12–December 24, 1987

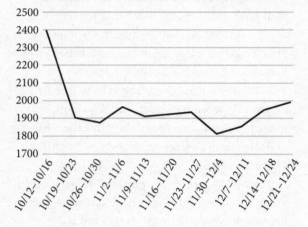

1. The central idea of this passage is primarily concerned with the

   A) ways in which digital communication have affected stock trading.

   B) manner in which international financial markets are intertwined.

   C) consequences of rapid growth in United States financial markets.

   D) circumstances that led to the stock market crash of 1987 and its aftermath.

2. With which of the following statements would the author most likely agree?

   A) There were no real consequences to investors following the stock market crash of October 1987.

   B) Globalization of financial markets has had a mostly negative effect on modernized financial industries.

   C) Stock traders should have seen the signs of an impending financial crisis in the months leading to the October 1987 crash.

   D) Financial experts should study human and computer viruses to understand how financial crises spread from one market to another.

3. Which choice provides the best evidence for the answer to the previous question?

   A) Lines 4-6 ("Daily gains … per day")

   B) Lines 25-27 ("While growth … dangerous")

   C) Lines 57-60 ("Investors watched … computer network")

   D) Lines 64-66 ("Fewer than two years … pre-crash highs")

4. Paragraph 1 (lines 1-9) most strongly suggests that

   A) Asian markets are more volatile than United States markets.

   B) slight fluctuations in the stock market are not cause for alarm.

   C) the S&P 500 is more stable than the New York Stock Exchange.

   D) a major crash like the one that occurred on Black Monday will never happen again.

5. As used in line 12, "immune" most nearly means

   A) inclined.

   B) problematic.

   C) resistant.

   D) sensitive.

6. According to paragraph 4, which of the following was a warning sign of Black Monday?

   A) The loss of 500 points in the Dow Jones Industrial Average

   B) Large losses in several international markets

   C) The announcement that measures would be taken to stabilize the United States dollar

   D) The development of digital communications allowing traders to monitor foreign markets

7. The author mentions the New Zealand stock market in lines 48-49 to

   A) explain how the instability of the Asian financial markets affected United States stocks.

   B) show how quickly the financial crisis spread from country to country on October 19, 1987.

   C) illustrate the fact that markets in other countries suffered larger losses than those in the United States did.

   D) provide an example of how the markets in other countries were affected by the global financial crisis.

8. The passage most strongly suggests that the New York traders' sense of panic on October 19, 1987, occurred because the traders

   A) had access to information about declining foreign markets through television reports.

   B) were unsure if they would be able to sell stocks they had purchased from other countries.

   C) did not know about the safeguards the government put in place to help avoid a financial crisis.

   D) knew that the market was going to suffer a huge collapse because of the preceding period of rapid growth.

9. Which choice provides the best evidence for the answer to the previous question?

   A) Lines 10-14 ("Black Monday ... the Great Depression")

   B) Lines 18-21 ("The world's financial markets ... around the world")

   C) Lines 39-42 ("Digital communication ... reports on television")

   D) Lines 50-52 ("When the opening bell ... to sell")

10. As used in line 71, "uniformity" most nearly means

    A) agreement.

    B) fairness.

    C) resemblance.

    D) standardization.

11. Data in the graph provide most direct support for which idea in the passage?

   A) The Dow Jones Industrial Average finished down over 500 points on Black Monday.

   B) The Dow Jones Industrial Average increased almost 50 percent in the months preceding Black Monday.

   C) The New Zealand stock market fell 60 percent in the days preceding Black Monday.

   D) United States stock markets surpassed their pre-crash highs fewer than two years after Black Monday.

ANSWERS & EXPLANATIONS

1. D
2. C
3. B
4. B
5. C
6. B
7. D
8. A
9. C
10. D
11. A

1. D
Difficulty: Medium

Category: Reading / Global

Strategic Advice: Review your Passage Map notes about the passage's central idea. Select the answer choice that correctly reflects your summary of the passage. Eliminate answer choices that contain details that support the central idea but do not state it.

Getting to the Answer: This passage is primarily about the events surrounding the stock market crash of 1987. Choice (D) is correct.

2. C
Difficulty: Hard

Category: Reading / Rhetoric

Strategic Advice: Select the answer choice that is directly supported by evidence in the passage. Avoid answer choices that are related to details presented in the text but go too far beyond its scope.

Getting to the Answer: In paragraph 3, the author states that "savvy traders know that rapid growth can be dangerous" (lines 26-27). Choice (C) is correct because it offers a logical conclusion based on the author's statement about savvy traders: They should have seen the signs of the impending crisis.

3. B
Difficulty: Medium

Category: Reading / Command of Evidence

Strategic Advice: Review how you selected the answer choice to the previous question. Then, determine which quotation most clearly supports that answer.

Getting to the Answer: As cited in the previous question's explanation, the author states that "savvy traders know that rapid growth can be dangerous" (lines 26-27). Choice (B) is correct because it features this phrase and therefore provides the best evidence for the answer to the previous question.

4. B
Difficulty: Medium

Category: Reading / Inference

Strategic Advice: Review your Passage Map notes for paragraph 1. The correct answer will be a conclusion clearly drawn from the information in the passage.

Getting to the Answer: In paragraph 1, the author explains that small gains and losses in the stock market over the course of a day are normal. You can infer that these small fluctuations are not a cause for alarm. Choice (B) is correct.

5. C

Difficulty: Medium

Category: Reading / Vocab-in-Context

Strategic Advice: Pretend the cited word is a blank in the sentence. Then, predict a word that could be substituted for that blank. Select the answer choice that best matches your prediction.

Getting to the Answer: The sentence to which the cited word belongs states that "Black Monday was the first event of its kind" (line 10) because people thought the modernized stock market was "immune" to severe crashes. In this context, "immune" means "protected from" or "resistant." Choice (C) is correct.

6. B

Difficulty: Easy

Category: Reading / Detail

Strategic Advice: The correct answer will be directly stated in the passage. Avoid answers choices that are true but do not answer the specific question.

Getting to the Answer: In paragraph 3, the author describes several events that foreshadowed the impending stock market crash. One of these events was the large losses in several world markets on October 14, 1987. Choice (B) is correct.

7. D

Difficulty: Hard

Category: Reading / Rhetoric

Strategic Advice: Read around the cited lines to determine how the details support the central idea of the overall passage.

Getting to the Answer: In the preceding sentence, the author explains that global investors responding to falling Asian markets attempted to sell their inventory, but there were not enough buyers. The author proceeds to explain that this created a "cascade in stock markets" (line 48), stating that the New Zealand market fell 60 percent, which illustrates the effect of the global financial crisis on other countries. Choice (D) is correct.

8. A

Difficulty: Medium

Category: Reading / Inference

Strategic Advice: When a question stem does not provide line numbers but does cite a detail from the passage, locate that detail to research the answer to the question.

Getting to the Answer: The author mentions the New York traders' panic in paragraph 5. In the previous paragraph, the author explains that the traders were able to watch reports of crashing Asian markets on television over the weekend leading to Black Monday. You can infer that the traders' access to this information instilled a sense of panic. Choice (A) is correct.

9. C

Difficulty: Medium

Category: Reading / Command of Evidence

Strategic Advice: Review how you selected the answer to the previous question. Eliminate answer choices that support incorrect answer choices for the previous question.

Getting to the Answer: In paragraph 4, the author explains that even though digital communication was not as sophisticated as it is today, traders were still able to watch the markets around the world fall apart, which likely led to the sense of panic the author describes in paragraph 5. Choice (C) is correct.

10. D

Difficulty: Medium

Category: Reading / Vocab-in-Context

Strategic Advice: Use other words in the sentence to which the cited word belongs to make a prediction.

Getting to the Answer: The author writes that "regulators overhauled trade-clearing protocols to bring uniformity to all prominent market products" (lines 69-71). "Regulators," therefore, promote "uniformity." Use "regulation" as your prediction. "Regulation" best matches "standardization," which means (D) is correct.

11. A

Difficulty: Medium

Category: Reading / Synthesis

Strategic Advice: Pay attention to an infographic's title, as it can help you eliminate irrelevant answer choices.

Getting to the Answer: The title of the graph is "Weekly DIJA: October 12–December 24, 1987," so you can eliminate any answer choices that refer to events or data outside this time frame. Eliminate B, which refers to the months preceding Black Monday, and D, which alludes to two years after Black Monday. You can also eliminate C because it refers to the New Zealand stock market. Choice (A) is therefore correct.

READING PRACTICE SET 3

Questions 1-10 are based on the following passage.

In this passage, American author Mark Twain recalls his boyhood in a small town along the Mississippi River.

My father was a justice of the peace, and I supposed he possessed the power of life and death over all men and could hang anybody that offended him.
Line This was distinction enough for me as a general
5 thing; but the desire to be a steamboatman kept intruding, nevertheless. I first wanted to be a cabin boy so that I could come out with a white apron on and shake a tablecloth over the side, where all my old comrades could see me. Later I thought I would
10 rather be the deck hand who stood on the end of the stage plank with a coil of rope in his hand, because he was particularly conspicuous.

But these were only daydreams—too heavenly to be contemplated as real possibilities. By and by
15 one of the boys went away. He was not heard of for a long time. At last he turned up as an apprentice engineer or "striker" on a steamboat. This thing shook the bottom out of all my Sunday-school teachings. That boy had been notoriously worldly,
20 and I had been just the reverse—yet he was exalted to this eminence, and I was left in obscurity and misery. There was nothing generous about this fellow in his greatness. He would always manage to have a rusty bolt to scrub while his boat was docked
25 at our town, and he would sit on the inside guard and scrub it, where we could all see him and envy him and loathe him.

He used all sorts of steamboat technicalities in his talk, as if he were so used to them that he forgot
30 common people could not understand them. He would speak of the "labboard" side of a horse in an easy, natural way that would make you wish he was dead. And he was always talking about "St. Looy" like an old citizen. Two or three of the
35 boys had long been persons of consideration among us because they had been to St. Louis once and had a vague general knowledge of its wonders, but the day of their glory was over now. They lapsed into a humble silence and learned to disappear when the
40 ruthless "cub" engineer approached. This fellow had money, too, and hair oil, and he wore a showy brass watch chain, a leather belt, and used no suspenders. No girl could withstand his charms. He "cut out" every boy in the village. When his boat blew up at
45 last, it diffused a tranquil contentment among us such as we had not known for months. But when he came home the next week, alive, renowned, and appeared in church all battered up and bandaged, a shining hero, stared at and wondered over by
50 everybody, it seemed to us that the partiality of Providence for an undeserving reptile had reached a point where it was open to criticism.

This creature's career could produce but one result, and it speedily followed. Boy after boy
55 managed to get on the river. Four sons of the chief merchant, and two sons of the county judge became pilots, the grandest position of all. But some of us could not get on the river—at least our parents would not let us.

60 So by and by I ran away. I said I would never come home again till I was a pilot and could return in glory. But somehow I could not manage it. I went meekly aboard a few of the boats that lay packed together like sardines at the long St. Louis wharf
65 and very humbly inquired for the pilots but got only a cold shoulder and short words from mates and clerks. I had to make the best of this sort of treatment for the time being, but I had comforting daydreams of a future when I should be a great and
70 honored pilot, with plenty of money, and could kill some of these mates and clerks and pay for them.

1. The central idea of the passage is that

   A) becoming a justice of the peace commanded the respect of others.

   B) the narrator eventually found work on a steamboat.

   C) working on a steamboat was the best thing the narrator could imagine as a child.

   D) the engineer didn't deserve the sympathy of others.

2. The passage most strongly suggests that the narrator thinks

   A) that the engineer's success is an injustice.

   B) a person must have deep religious beliefs.

   C) being a deck hand pays the highest wages.

   D) that steamboat work will make him famous.

3. Which choice provides the best evidence for the answer to the previous question?

   A) Lines 9-12 ("Later I thought … conspicuous")

   B) Lines 17-22 ("This thing shook … and misery")

   C) Lines 53-54 ("This creature's career … followed")

   D) Lines 57-59 ("But some … let us")

4. Which of the following best describes the relationship between the engineer and the other boys in the town?

   A) The engineer is envious of the other boys.

   B) The other boys are envious of the engineer.

   C) The engineer thinks he is better than the other boys.

   D) The other boys think they are better than the engineer.

5. The narrator's statement in lines 1-3 ("I supposed he … offended them.") primarily suggests the

   A) power held by a justice of the peace in a frontier town.

   B) respect in which the townspeople held his father and how that influenced his thinking.

   C) somewhat naïve point of view he held about his father's importance.

   D) harsh environment in which he was brought up and how that influenced his point of view.

6. As used in line 4, "distinction" most nearly means

   A) difference.

   B) feature.

   C) clarity.

   D) prestige.

7. The narrator refers to "steamboat technicalities" in lines 28-30 ("He used … understand them.") to

   A) emphasize the engineer's desire to appear sophisticated.

   B) convey the engineer's strong interest in steamboat work.

   C) show the engineer's inability to communicate effectively.

   D) reveal the engineer's fascination with trivial information.

8. As used in line 35, "consideration" most nearly means

   A) generosity.

   B) reputation.

   C) contemplation.

   D) unselfishness.

9. It can be most reasonably inferred that the boys in the town

   A) had all gone to St. Louis before.

   B) had all gone to Sunday school.

   C) were relieved when the boat blew up.

   D) were in competition with one another.

10. Which choice provides the best evidence for the answer to the previous question?

    A) Lines 13-14 ("But these … real possibilities")

    B) Lines 44-46 ("When his boat … for months")

    C) Lines 46-49 ("But when he … a shining hero")

    D) Lines 55-57 ("Four sons … grandest position of all")

ANSWERS & EXPLANATIONS

1. C
2. A
3. B
4. B
5. C
6. D
7. A
8. B
9. C
10. B

1. C
Difficulty: Medium

Category: Reading / Global

Strategic Advice: Look at any common words or themes in your Passage Map to determine the central idea of the passage.

Getting to the Answer: The narrator references his desire to be a "steamboatman" (line 5) throughout the entire passage. Watch out for B: even though the narrator wants to work on a steamboat, the passage never states that he eventually did so. Choice (C) is correct.

2. A
Difficulty: Hard

Category: Reading / Inference

Strategic Advice: Eliminate any answer choices that cannot be directly concluded from the facts in the passage.

Getting to the Answer: The narrator expresses his disdain for the engineer throughout the passage, beginning in the second paragraph, in which the narrator writes, "There was nothing generous about this fellow in his greatness" (lines 22-23). The remainder of the passage details the tense relationship between the engineer and the other boys in town, including the narrator. Choice (A) is correct.

3. B
Difficulty: Hard

Category: Reading / Command of Evidence

Strategic Advice: Use the parts of the passage you used to answer the previous question to help you eliminate incorrect answer choices to a Command of Evidence question.

Getting to the Answer: Even though the narrator discusses his dislike of the engineer throughout the passage, the correct answer to the previous question specifically stated that the narrator thought the engineer's success was an injustice. Eliminate A and D because neither quotation directly mentions the engineer. The quotation in C mentions the engineer, but refers to a result of the engineer's career path, so you can eliminate this answer choice. Choice (B) details the narrator's initial reaction to the engineer's success and is therefore correct.

4. B
Difficulty: Medium

Category: Reading / Inference

Strategic Advice: Pay attention to how characters view themselves and other characters as you read a U.S. and World Literature passage.

Getting to the Answer: Though the narrator may think he is better than the engineer, the relationship is best described in terms of envy. The narrator and the other boys wish they could have a job like the engineer does. The last two paragraphs provide evidence of this, as "[b]oy after boy managed to get on the river" (lines 54-55). Choice (B) is correct.

5. C

Difficulty: Medium

Category: Reading / Inference

Strategic Advice: Read around cited lines to draw a logical conclusion from what's stated in the passage.

Getting to the Answer: Lines 1-3 convey the narrator's boyish, naïve belief that his father was all-powerful in his role as justice of the peace; they help establish that all events described in the passage will reflect the point of view of a child.

6. D

Difficulty: Easy

Category: Reading / Vocab-in-Context

Strategic Advice: The correct answer choice will be synonymous with the cited word as it is used in context but not necessarily other common meanings of that word.

Getting to the Answer: The context of the passage makes it clear that the narrator thought his father possessed "the power of life and death over all men" (lines 2-3), which indicates respect or status. Choice (D), "prestige," is correct.

7. A

Difficulty: Medium

Category: Reading / Rhetoric

Strategic Advice: When a question stem contains the phrase "in order to," determine why the author or narrator included the part of the passage cited.

Getting to the Answer: The cited phrase is part of a description of the steamboat engineer, whom the narrator dislikes. The next sentence after the one cited in the question stem says the engineer would apply "steamboat technicalities"

to non-steamboat contexts in a "way that would make you wish he was dead" (lines 32-33). The engineer was clearly determined to impress others with his knowledge of steamboat work, which matches (A).

8. B

Difficulty: Medium

Category: Reading / Vocab-in-Context

Strategic Advice: Pretend the cited word is a blank in the sentence and predict a synonym that can replace it. Select which choice best matches your prediction.

Getting to the Answer: The context in which "consideration" appears implies the boys were known for being familiar with and knowing a good deal about St. Louis. Choice (B), "reputation," is correct.

9. C

Difficulty: Hard

Category: Reading / Inference

Strategic Advice: Avoid answer choices to Inference questions that go beyond the scope of what is stated in the passage.

Getting to the Answer: The narrator states that when the engineer's boat blew up, "it diffused a tranquil contentment among us such as we had not known for months" (lines 45-46). You can infer that this "tranquil contentment" was a sort of "relief," which matches (C).

10. B

Difficulty: Medium

Category: Reading / Command of Evidence

Strategic Advice: Avoid answer choices that contain lines from the passage that are far removed from where you found the answer to the previous question.

Getting to the Answer: The phrase "diffused a tranquil contentment" in line 45 supports the correct answer to the previous question, which states that the boys were relieved when the boat blew up. Choice (B) contains this phrase and is therefore correct.

READING PRACTICE SET 4

Questions 1-11 are based on the following passage.

This passage is from the Declaration of Independence, drafted by Thomas Jefferson between June 11 and 28, 1776, and adopted by the Continental Congress on July 4th of that year.

When in the Course of human events, it
becomes necessary for one people to dissolve the
political bands which have connected them with
Line another, and to assume among the powers of the
5 earth, the separate and equal station to which the
Laws of Nature and of Nature's God entitle them, a
decent respect to the opinions of mankind requires
that they should declare the causes which impel
them to the separation.
10 We hold these truths to be self-evident, that all
men are created equal, that they are endowed by
their Creator with certain unalienable Rights, that
among these are Life, Liberty and the pursuit of
Happiness.—That to secure these rights, Govern-
15 ments are instituted among Men, deriving their just
powers from the consent of the governed, —That
whenever any Form of Government becomes
destructive of these ends, it is the Right of the
People to alter or to abolish it, and to institute new
20 Government, laying its foundation on such principles and organizing its powers in such form, as
to them shall seem most likely to effect their Safety
and Happiness. Prudence, indeed, will dictate
that Governments long established should not be
25 changed for light and transient causes; and accord-
ingly all experience hath shewn, that mankind are
more disposed to suffer, while evils are sufferable,
than to right themselves by abolishing the forms to
which they are accustomed. But when a long train
30 of abuses and usurpations, pursuing invariably the
same Object evinces a design to reduce them under
absolute Despotism, it is their right, it is their duty,
to throw off such Government, and to provide new
Guards for their future security.—Such has been

35 the patient sufferance of these Colonies; and such
is now the necessity which constrains them to alter
their former Systems of Government. The history
of the present King of Great Britain is a history
of repeated injuries and usurpations, all having
40 in direct object the establishment of an absolute
Tyranny over these States. To prove this, let Facts be
submitted to a candid world.
In every stage of these Oppressions We have
Petitioned for Redress in the most humble terms:
45 Our repeated Petitions have been answered only by
repeated injury. A Prince whose character is thus
marked by every act which may define a Tyrant, is
unfit to be the ruler of a free people.
Nor have We been wanting in attentions to our
50 British brethren. We have warned them from time
to time of attempts by their legislature to extend
an unwarrantable jurisdiction over us. We have
reminded them of the circumstances of our emi-
gration and settlement here. We have appealed to
55 their native justice and magnanimity, and we have
conjured them by the ties of our common kindred
to disavow these usurpations, which, would inevita-
bly interrupt our connections and correspondence.
They too have been deaf to the voice of justice and
60 of consanguinity. We must, therefore, acquiesce in
the necessity, which denounces our Separation, and
hold them, as we hold the rest of mankind, Enemies
in War, in Peace Friends.
We, therefore, the Representatives of the united
65 States of America, in General Congress, Assembled,
appealing to the Supreme Judge of the world for the
rectitude of our intentions, do, in the Name, and
by Authority of the good People of these Colonies,
solemnly publish and declare, That these United
70 Colonies are, and of Right ought to be Free and
Independent States; that they are Absolved from
all Allegiance to the British Crown, and that all
political connection between them and the State of
Great Britain, is and ought to be totally dissolved;
75 and that as Free and Independent States, they have
full Power to levy War, conclude Peace, contract

Alliances, establish Commerce, and to do all other Acts and Things which Independent States may of right do. And for the support of this Declaration,
80 with a firm reliance on the protection of divine Providence, we mutually pledge to each other our Lives, our Fortunes and our sacred Honor.

1. Which statement expresses one of the central ideas of the passage?

   A) Government should not be changed "for light and transient causes" (line 25).

   B) Colonists have experienced "patient sufferance," hoping for change (line 35).

   C) There have been "repeated Petitions" to the King but to no avail (line 45).

   D) All people have the right to "Life, Liberty, and the pursuit of Happiness" (lines 13-14).

2. Based on the creation of this document, it can be reasonably inferred that

   A) Jefferson and the other founding fathers were rebellious by nature.

   B) the injustices inflicted upon the colonies had taken place for at least a year.

   C) the colonists' requests for changes had made matters worse.

   D) Jefferson hoped the King would modify his policies upon receiving the document.

3. Which choice provides the best evidence for the answer to the previous question?

   A) Lines 23-25 ("Prudence ... transient causes")

   B) Lines 43-46 ("In every stage ... repeated injury")

   C) Lines 52-54 ("We have ... settlement here")

   D) Lines 69-74 ("That these ... totally dissolved")

4. The first paragraph can best be described as

   A) an illustration of Jefferson's skill as a lawyer.

   B) a theory about what makes good government.

   C) an introduction stating the reason for the document.

   D) a list of specific complaints against Great Britain.

5. Jefferson's use of the term "self-evident" in line 10 to describe certain "truths" implies that

   A) the absence of these truths is unnatural.

   B) self-government is the preferred form of government.

   C) those who do not believe in these truths are foolish.

   D) the only true way to live is to be happy.

6. As used in line 40, "absolute" most nearly means

   A) doubtless.

   B) fixed.

   C) conclusive.

   D) total.

7. According to paragraph 2, when a government destroys its citizens' rights, those citizens should

   A) appeal to the governments of other countries.

   B) change or get rid of that government.

   C) emigrate to another country.

   D) sue the government for abuse of power.

8. As used in line 42, "candid" most nearly means

   A) impartial.

   B) unrehearsed.

   C) straightforward.

   D) outspoken.

9. In the fourth paragraph, Jefferson addresses the counterclaim that the

   A) British people will find the actions of the King unjust.

   B) British people will condemn the colonists for declaring independence.

   C) King will declare war on the colonies.

   D) King will take action against those who are sympathetic toward the colonies.

10. Jefferson would likely view the relationship between the colonists and the British people as

    A) irreconcilable.

    B) fraught with mistrust.

    C) damaged, but not irreversibly so.

    D) based on mutual respect.

11. Which choice provides the best evidence for the answer to the previous question?

    A) Lines 29-34 ("But when … future security")

    B) Lines 37-39 ("The history … usurpations")

    C) Lines 62-63 ("Enemies in … Friends")

    D) Lines 79-82 ("And for the support … Honor")

ANSWERS & EXPLANATIONS

1. D
2. C
3. B
4. C
5. A
6. D
7. B
8. A
9. B
10. C
11. C

1. D
Difficulty: Easy

Category: Reading / Global

Strategic Advice: Compare the answer choices to see if one of them conveys a larger idea than the others.

Getting to the Answer: Though every answer choice reflects an idea stated in the passage, think critically about which idea is truly central, and permeates the passage. Though A, B, and C are all mentioned in the passage, they are not revisited by the author and, therefore, cannot constitute central ideas. Remember, details mentioned in passing will never be the central idea of a passage. Choice (D) describes one of the central ideas Jefferson conveys in this important document, as it is revisited multiple times throughout.

2. C
Difficulty: Hard

Category: Reading / Inference

Strategic Advice: Avoid answer choices that appear to be probable but are not supported by evidence in the passage.

Getting to the Answer: Jefferson outlines the grievances that led to the creation of this document. In the third paragraph, he suggests that whenever the colonists petitioned for change, the King inflicted additional acts of tyranny. This clearly made the situation worse for the colonists. Therefore, (C) is correct. Choices A and D go beyond the information in the passage, which does not detail whether Jefferson had a rebellious nature, or what his hopes would be upon the King's receiving of this document.

3. B
Difficulty: Medium

Category: Reading / Command of Evidence

Strategic Advice: Avoid answer choices that provide evidence to incorrect answer choices to the previous question.

Getting to the Answer: To answer the previous question, you used information in the third paragraph that demonstrated how colonists were abused when they asked for changes. Choice (B) cites these lines and is therefore correct.

4. C
Difficulty: Medium

Category: Reading / Rhetoric

Strategic Advice: Consider how the cited paragraph functions in relation to the rest of the passage.

Getting to the Answer: Choice A is incorrect because while a reader may be impressed by Jefferson's literary abilities, this is not a legal document to be presented in a courtroom, and has nothing to do with Jefferson's skills as an attorney. Choice D is incorrect because the first paragraph doesn't begin listing grievances or describing an ideal government. The first paragraph sets the stage for the rest of the document by introducing Jefferson's reasons for writing it. It outlines the fact that a separation is necessary between the colonies and mentions that the reasons for that separation will be outlined in the rest of the document. Choice (C) matches this summary.

5. A
Difficulty: Hard

Category: Reading / Rhetoric

Strategic Advice: Look at the context of the cited phrase to determine its meaning and how it is used to aid the passage's rhetoric.

Getting to the Answer: The "truths" Jefferson lists include the equality of all people and the fact that humans have certain rights that cannot be taken away. Because he doesn't provide reasons for these truths, "self-evident" suggests these truths are somehow obvious in the world Jefferson lives in. If the presence of these truths is obvious, their absence would be quite strange. Choice (A) matches this prediction. Watch out for B, which describes something that Jefferson believes, but which doesn't relate to the cited lines.

6. D
Difficulty: Medium

Category: Reading / Vocab-in-Context

Strategic Advice: Don't automatically pick a definition that you are familiar with; make a prediction and select the answer choice that best matches your prediction.

Getting to the Answer: Jefferson accuses the King of Great Britain of "absolute Despotism,"

(line 32) or tyranny. Absolute is modifying Despotism in order to describe the extent or reach. In this case, the King exerted his power and rule in both Great Britain and the American Colonies. "Total" is an appropriate synonym for this far-reaching control. Choice (D) is therefore correct.

7. B
Difficulty: Easy

Category: Reading / Detail

Strategic Advice: Use your Passage Map to locate a detail cited in a question stem without a line number.

Getting to the Answer: Jefferson states that it is the "Right of the People to alter or abolish" (lines 18-19) the government if the "truths" he has described are destroyed. "Altering" or "abolishing" the government means to "change" or "get rid of." Choice (B) matches this prediction and is therefore correct.

8. A
Difficulty: Medium

Category: Reading / Vocab-in-Context

Strategic Advice: Avoid common definitions, and make a prediction for the cited word in the context of the passage before selecting an answer.

Getting to the Answer: In this document, Jefferson is exposing the King of Great Britain's treatment of the colonies. He writes, "let Facts be submitted to a candid world" (lines 41-42) implying his hope that the world will evaluate these facts. Jefferson is most likely hoping for a fair assessment of the facts, which he believes will favor his position. In this context, it makes the most sense that he assumes—and hopes—that the rest of the world will be "impartial" or "fair" in their judgment. Therefore, (A) is correct.

9. B

Difficulty: Hard

Category: Reading / Rhetoric

Strategic Advice: When analyzing a counter-claim, keep in mind the point of view, or opinion, that the author would have toward those who disagree with him.

Getting to the Answer: Think about who is most likely to disagree with Jefferson. While you know the King is going to oppose him, the British monarch is not mentioned in the fourth paragraph. Rather, Jefferson is anticipating that the British people will denounce "our Separation" (line 61), suggesting he doesn't think the residents of Great Britain will appreciate the colonies' declaring independence. Choice C is incorrect because although history proves that the King ultimately did declare war, this goes outside the scope of the paragraph and passage. Choice (B) is correct.

10. C

Difficulty: Hard

Category: Reading / Rhetoric

Strategic Advice: Look carefully for phrases that indicate Jefferson's feelings toward the British people.

Getting to the Answer: Though Jefferson is obviously disappointed at the lack of response from "our British brethren" (lines 49-50), he does not seem to view the relationship as entirely broken. You can quickly eliminate D, which is positive, and A, because Jefferson never says that the situation is beyond repair. While the colonists and the British people may not like one another, there is no evidence that they mistrust each other. While Jefferson and the King may never be able to overcome their differences, the former clearly hopes that this hostility does not apply to the entire British population. Choice (C) is correct.

11. C

Difficulty: Medium

Category: Reading / Command of Evidence

Strategic Advice: Use any notes that helped you answer the previous question to locate the part of the passage that provides the best evidence for the previous answer.

Getting to the Answer: To correctly answer the previous question, you examined the end of the fourth paragraph in which Jefferson calls the British people "Enemies in War, in Peace Friends" (lines 62-63). From this statement, you can infer that Jefferson sees the relationship between the colonists and the British people as being temporarily broken while war rages; however, once the conflict is resolved, the relationship will mend itself. Therefore, (C) is correct.

READING PRACTICE SET 5

Questions 1-11 are based on the following passage and supplementary material.

The following passage discusses the possibility that there is life on Mars. Interest in the subject reached a peak when NASA sent two unmanned spacecraft to Mars in 1975. After 10 months, Vikings 1 and 2 entered orbits around The Red Planet and released landers.

When the first of the two *Viking* landers touched down on Martian soil on July 20, 1976, and began to send camera images back to Earth, the scientists
Line at the Jet Propulsion Laboratory (J.P.L.) could not
5 suppress a certain nervous anticipation, like people who hold a ticket to a lottery they have a one-in-a-million chance of winning. The first photographs that arrived, however, did not contain any evidence of life. What revealed itself to them was merely a
10 barren landscape littered with rocks and boulders. The view resembled nothing so much as a flat section of desert—in fact, the winning entry in a contest at J.P.L. for the photograph most accurately predicting what Mars would look like was a
15 snapshot taken in a particularly arid section of the Mojave Desert.

The scientists were soon ready to turn their attention from visible life to microorganisms. The twin *Viking* landers carried three experiments
20 designed to detect current biological activity and one to detect organic compounds, because researchers thought it possible that life had developed on early Mars just as it is thought to have developed on Earth, through the gradual chemical evolution
25 of complex organic molecules. To detect biological activity, Martian soil samples were treated with various nutrients that would produce characteristic by-products if life-forms were active in the soil. The results from all three experiments were inconclu-
30 sive. The fourth experiment heated a soil sample to look for signs of organic material but found none, an unexpected result because at least organic compounds from the steady bombardment of the

Martian surface by meteorites were thought to have
35 been present.

The absence of organic materials, some scientists speculated, was the result of intense ultraviolet radiation penetrating the atmosphere of Mars and destroying organic compounds in the soil.
40 Although Mars's atmosphere still has a high percentage of carbon dioxide, the density of the carbon dioxide used to be greater, thus protecting the surface from harmful rays of the sun. Gradually, this concentration thinned as more carbon dioxide
45 was converted into rock. This means that even if life had gotten a start on early Mars, it could not have survived the exposure to ultraviolet radiation when the atmosphere thinned. Mars never developed a protective layer of ozone as Earth did.
50 Despite the disappointing *Viking* results, there are those who still keep open the possibility of life on Mars. They point out that the *Viking* data cannot be considered the final word on Martian life because the two landers only sampled two limited—and
55 uninteresting—sites. The *Viking* landing sites were not chosen for what they might tell of the planet's biology. They were chosen primarily because they appeared to be safe for landing a spacecraft. The landing sites were on parts of the Martian plains
60 that appeared relatively featureless from orbital photographs. The type of Martian terrain that these researchers suggest may be a possible hiding place for active life has an earthly parallel: the ice-free region of southern Victoria Land, Antarctica,
65 where the temperatures in some dry valleys average below zero. Organisms known as endoliths, a form of blue-green algae that has adapted to this harsh environment, were found living inside certain translucent, porous rocks in these Antarctic valleys.
70 The argument based on this discovery is that if life did exist on early Mars, it is possible that it escaped worsening conditions by similarly seeking refuge in rocks. Skeptics object, however, stating that Mars in its present state is simply too dry, even compared
75 with Antarctic valleys, to sustain any life whatsoever.

Should Mars eventually prove to be completely barren of life, as some suspect, then this would have a significant impact on the current view of the chemical origin of life. It could be much more
80 difficult to get life started on a planet than scientists thought before the *Viking* landings.

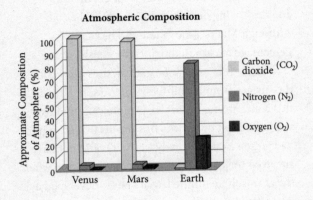

1. The researchers' argument that life may exist in Martian rocks rests on the idea that

    A) life evolved in the same way on two different planets.

    B) organisms may adopt similar properties in similar environments.

    C) the Viking landers collected rock samples from only two sites.

    D) carbon dioxide indicates the presence of life.

2. Which choice provides the best evidence for the answer to the previous question?

    A) Lines 11-16 ("The view ... Mojave Desert")

    B) Lines 18-25 ("The twin *Viking* landers ... molecules")

    C) Lines 55-57 ("The *Viking* ... planet's biology")

    D) Lines 43-45 ("Gradually ... into rock")

3. The passage suggests that an important difference between Mars and Earth is that, unlike Earth, Mars

    A) accumulated organic compounds in its soil.

    B) lies in the path of harmful rays of ultraviolet radiation.

    C) once possessed an atmosphere with a dense concentration of carbon dioxide.

    D) could not sustain any life that developed early on.

4. Which choice provides the best evidence for the answer to the previous question?

    A) Lines 9-10 ("What revealed ... boulders")

    B) Lines 40-43 ("Although ... the sun")

    C) Lines 45-48 ("This means ... thinned")

    D) Lines 66-69 ("Organisms ... Antarctic valleys")

5. In describing the scientists' reaction to the *Viking* images of Mars, the author's reference to the lottery (lines 5-7) implies that

    A) there was cause for celebration, just as there would be if a person won the lottery.

    B) the scientists couldn't believe what they were seeing in the images.

    C) there was little chance that the images would show something conclusive.

    D) the anticipation level was inappropriate for the occasion of scientific research.

6. According to the passage, the surface of Mars most resembles

A) the ice valleys of Antarctica.

B) a very dry section of a desert.

C) that of Earth's moon.

D) that of Earth, if it lacked its ozone layer.

7. As used in line 63, "active" most nearly means

A) moving.

B) energetic.

C) functional.

D) present.

8. The main purpose of the fourth paragraph (lines 50-75) is to indicate that

A) the Viking program was unsuccessful due to poor selection of landing sites.

B) the results of the Viking program do not necessarily prove that Mars is devoid of life.

C) the detection of life on Mars was not a primary objective of the Viking program.

D) scientists were not expecting to discover life on the Martian plains.

9. As used in line 54, "limited" most nearly means

A) imperfect.

B) restricted.

C) specific.

D) incomplete.

10. Which of the following facts from the passage is supported by the information in the graph?

A) Exposure to ultraviolet radiation lowered the carbon dioxide level in Mars's atmosphere.

B) Mars's atmosphere still has a high percentage of carbon dioxide.

C) The absence of organic materials points to a low nitrogen percentage in Mars's atmosphere.

D) The atmospheric composition of Mars resembles that of Earth.

11. Ozone is a gas composed entirely of oxygen molecules. What information in the graph supports the statement in the passage that Mars never developed a protective layer of ozone as Earth did?

A) Earth's atmosphere contains 20 percent oxygen.

B) The amount of nitrogen in the atmospheres of Venus and Mars is approximately the same.

C) Mars's atmosphere contains a very small percentage of oxygen.

D) Earth's atmosphere contains a very small percentage of carbon dioxide.

ANSWERS & EXPLANATIONS

1. A
2. B
3. D
4. C
5. C
6. B
7. C
8. B
9. A
10. B
11. C

1. A

Category: Reading / Inference

Difficulty: Hard

Strategic Advice: This question requires you to make an inference about an assumption held throughout the passage.

Getting to the Answer: Though researchers might have assumed certain ideas about the properties of organisms living in similar environments, thus making choice B seem possible, (A) is the correct answer. In the research described throughout the passage, there is an underlying assumption that life evolved in the same way on two different planets, Earth and Mars. The researchers also spell this assumption out clearly in the second sentence of paragraph 2. Choice (A) is correct.

2. B

Difficulty: Medium

Category: Reading / Command of Evidence

Strategic Advice: Retrace your steps in answering the previous question to locate the proper support for the correct answer.

Getting to the Answer: The most direct support for the answer to the previous question comes from the beginning of the second paragraph. Because (B) includes the statement that "researchers thought it possible that life had developed on early Mars just as it is thought to have developed on Earth," it is the best evidence to support the previous answer. Choice (B) is correct.

3. D

Category: Reading / Inference

Difficulty: Hard

Strategic Advice: Watch out for answer choices that may resonate with statements made in the passage but do not actually answer the question.

Getting to the Answer: Choices A and B could not be correct, as the passage describes the possibility that both of these attributes might be present on Mars and Earth—these are similarities, not differences. Likewise, C is incorrect, as the passage doesn't address the density level of carbon dioxide on Earth. The only answer choice that describes a difference suggested in the passage is (D); Mars could not sustain any life that developed early on due to the intense UV radiation that killed life forms on the surface. Choice (D) is correct.

4. C

Difficulty: Medium

Category: Reading / Command of Evidence

Strategic Advice: Review how you chose the answer to the previous question to help you determine which answer choice contains the best evidence.

Getting to the Answer: Look for the answer choice that shows why Mars could not support life, specifically because of the UV radiation. While A, B, and D are in the vicinity of the relevant information, only (C) demonstrates how the intense UV radiation made it impossible for Mars to sustain any life that developed early on. Choice (C) is correct.

5. C

Category: Reading / Rhetoric

Difficulty: Medium

Strategic Advice: Review your notes for the paragraph in which the reference occurs to put the statement in context.

Getting to the Answer: The author says that the scientists were like "people who hold a ticket to a lottery they have a one-in-a-million chance of winning" (lines 5-7). While it might be nice for the scientists to imagine a life of wealth, the author is clearly emphasizing how unlikely winning the lottery is and connecting this to the scientists. The extreme odds described in this reference imply that the author thinks there was little chance that the images of Mars would show something conclusive. Therefore, (C) is correct.

6. B

Category: Reading / Detail

Difficulty: Medium

Strategic Advice: The answer is stated explicitly in the passage, so make sure you don't select an answer choice that goes beyond the text.

Getting to the Answer: Though it might be inferred from the next-to-last paragraph that the surface of Mars resembles A, the ice valleys of Antarctica, the similarity is theoretical at best. In contrast, the last sentence of the first paragraph states that "the photograph most accurately predicting what Mars would look like was a snapshot taken from a particularly arid section of the Mojave Desert" (lines 13-16). Choice (B) is correct.

7. C

Difficulty: Medium

Category: Reading / Vocab-in-Context

Strategic Advice: Look for context clues in the target and surrounding sentences. Predict the meaning of the word and then look for a match in the answer choices.

Getting to the Answer: Scientists were testing soil from Mars for life-forms and performing some kind of action. Choice (C), functional, is a great match. Choice D, "present," fails to distinguish between life forms that were alive and the fossilized remains of past organisms. While physical motion may be a great clue that large organisms (like mammals) are alive, it doesn't necessarily apply to bacteria, ruling out choice A, as well. Choice (C) is correct.

8. B

Difficulty: Medium

Category: Reading / Rhetoric

Strategic Advice: As you revisit the fourth paragraph, consider the content, as well as *why* the author chose to include it. How does it support the overall idea of the passage?

Getting to the Answer: The fourth paragraph opens the door to the possibility of life on Mars. Without the fourth paragraph, readers might think that the Viking program conclusively eliminated any hope for the discovery of Martian life forms. Choice (B) is correct. Watch out for extreme answer choices or answer choices that use details from other parts of the passage. While the landing sites were not ideal, A goes too far by declaring the program unsuccessful. While D may be true, as the scientists were not expecting to find actual life forms, this idea is not conveyed in the fourth paragraph.

9. A

Difficulty: Medium

Category: Reading / Vocab-in-Context

Strategic Advice: Reread the sentence to make a prediction for the cited word as it is used in context.

Getting to the Answer: The paragraph in which this word appears states that the landers sampled material from locations that weren't necessarily the best sites to learn about Mars's biology. Based on this context, you can conclude that the testing sites were far from ideal. This is a great match for "imperfect," making (A) the correct answer.

10. B

Difficulty: Medium

Category: Reading / Synthesis

Strategic Advice: To answer this question, you must compare the information provided in the passage and the graph.

Getting to the Answer: While many of the answer choices listed may be supported by the passage, only one will be bolstered by the graph. The graph shows that Mars's atmosphere is approximately 95 percent carbon dioxide, thus supporting the passage's statement that "Mars's atmosphere still has a high percentage of carbon dioxide" (lines 40-41). Choice (B) is correct.

11. C

Difficulty: Hard

Category: Reading / Synthesis

Strategic Advice: Reread the question stem to make sure you understand what is being asked.

Getting to the Answer: You don't need to be a scientist to correctly answer this question. Because ozone is composed entirely of oxygen, there would need to be a significant level of this gas in order for ozone to form in a planet's atmosphere. Earth, according to the graph, has an atmosphere made up of 20 percent oxygen. However, the graph shows that Mars's atmosphere has only a small percentage of oxygen. This helps explain why Mars never developed an ozone layer. Choice (C) is correct.

READING PRACTICE SET 6

Questions 1-10 are based on the following passage.

The following passage is an excerpt from The Remains of the Day *by Kazuo Ishiguro. The novel, which won the Man Booker Prize for Fiction in 1989, is told from the point of view of a British butler.*

I had rarely had reason to enter my father's room prior to this occasion and I was newly struck by the smallness and starkness of it. Indeed, I recall my impression at the time was of having stepped into a
[5] prison cell, but then, this might have had as much to do with the pale early light as with the size of the room or the bareness of its walls. For my father had opened his curtains and was sitting, shaved and in full uniform, on the edge of his bed from where
[10] evidently he had been watching the sky turn to dawn. At least one assumed he had been watching the sky, there being little else to view from his small window other than roof-tiles and guttering. The oil lamp beside his bed had been extinguished, and
[15] when I saw my father glance disapprovingly at the lamp I had brought to guide me up the rickety staircase, I quickly lowered the wick. Having done this, I noticed all the more the effect of the pale light coming into the room and the way it lit up the edges
[20] of my father's craggy, lined, still awesome features.

"Ah," I said, and gave a short laugh, "I might have known Father would be up and ready for the day."

"I've been up for the past three hours," he said, looking me up and down rather coldly.

[25] "I hope Father is not being kept awake by his arthritic troubles."

"I get all the sleep I need."

My father reached forward to the only chair in the room, a small wooden one, and placing both
[30] hands on its back, brought himself to his feet. When I saw him stood upright before me, I could not be sure to what extent he was hunched over due to his infirmity and what extent due to the habit of accommodating the steeply sloped ceilings of the room.

[35] "I have come here to relate something to you, Father."

"Then relate it briefly and concisely. I haven't all morning to listen to your chatter."

"In that case, Father, I will come straight to the
[40] point."

"Come to the point then and be done with it. Some of us have work to be getting on with."

"Very well. Since you wish me to be brief, I will do my best to comply. The fact is, Father has
[45] become increasingly infirm. So much so that even the duties of the under-butler are now beyond his capabilities. His lordship is of the view, as indeed I am myself, that while Father is allowed to continue with his present round of duties, he represents an
[50] ever-present threat to the smooth running of this household, and in particular to next week's important international gathering."

My father's face, in the half-light, betrayed no emotion whatsoever.

[55] "Principally," I continued, "it has been felt that Father should no longer be asked to wait at table, whether or not guests are present."

"I have waited at table every day for the last fifty-four years," my father remarked, his voice perfectly
[60] unhurried.

"Furthermore, it has been decided that Father should not carry laden trays of any sort for even the shortest distance. In view of these limitations, and knowing Father's esteem for conciseness, I have
[65] listed here the revised round of duties he will from now on be expected to perform."

I felt disinclined actually to hand him the piece of paper I was holding, and so put it down on the end of his bed. My father glanced at it then
[70] returned his gaze to me. There was still no trace of emotion discernible in his expression, and his hands on the back of the chair appeared perfectly relaxed. Hunched over or not, it was impossible not to be reminded of the sheer impact of his physical
[75] presence.

1. The passage can best be described as

   A) a social commentary on working-class issues.

   B) an example of people failing to communicate fully.

   C) a description of a typical father-son relationship.

   D) a model for employee/employer communication.

2. In this passage, the narrator's tone can best be described as

   A) critical.

   B) sympathetic.

   C) ironic.

   D) restrained.

3. Which choice provides the best evidence for the answer to the previous question?

   A) Line 42 ("Some of us … on with")

   B) Lines 25-26 ("I hope … troubles")

   C) Lines 37-38 ("Then relate it … chatter")

   D) Lines 53-54 ("My father's … whatsoever")

4. The narrator's feelings about his father can best be described as

   A) nervously awed.

   B) bitterly condescending.

   C) wistfully disappointed.

   D) coldly callous.

5. Which choice provides the best evidence for the answer to the previous question?

   A) Lines 13-20 ("The oil lamp … features")

   B) Lines 30-34 ("When I … of the room")

   C) Lines 39-40 ("In that case … the point")

   D) Lines 55-57 ("Principally … are present")

6. The narrator is surprised by the "small-ness and starkness," mentioned in line 3, of his father's room because

   A) his father is a large man.

   B) he thinks his father deserves better.

   C) he hasn't visited the room very often.

   D) his room is much bigger and not as plain.

7. As used in lines 33-34, "accommodating" most nearly means

   A) indulging.

   B) accepting.

   C) adjusting to.

   D) providing for.

8. As used in line 35 and line 37, "relate" most nearly means

   A) associate.

   B) connect.

   C) apply.

   D) tell.

9. The narrator's addressing his father in the third person in lines 44-52 and 61-66 serves to

A) demonstrate how hard it is to have a father and son working together as butlers.

B) allow the narrator to demonstrate tremendous respect for his father.

C) reinforce the intense formality and coldness of the father-son relationship.

D) suggest how angry the narrator actually is at his father's coldness.

10. The father's response to receiving the news in the final paragraph (lines 67-75) can best be described as

A) sympathetic.

B) emotionless.

C) proud.

D) responsive.

ANSWERS & EXPLANATIONS

1. B

2. D

3. D

4. A

5. A

6. C

7. C

8. D

9. C

10. B

1. B
Difficulty: Medium

Category: Reading / Global

Strategic Advice: Avoid answer choices that may sound impressive but are not reflective of the best way to describe the passage.

Getting to the Answer: Throughout this passage, two men have a conversation, yet they fail to directly convey their feelings to each other, making choice C incorrect. There isn't enough information to describe the passage as a social commentary on working-class issues, so A is incorrect. Likewise, D offers a description that is much too upbeat to reflect the content of the passage. Choice (B) is correct.

2. D
Difficulty: Hard

Category: Reading / Rhetoric

Strategic Advice: In a U.S. and World Literature passage, the term "tone" refers to attitude or point of view.

Getting to the Answer: Although you may feel that the father is critical, that doesn't mean that the overall tone of the passage is, so eliminate A. Few emotions are suggested in this passage; instead, it is the reader who is left to feel a certain way about the characters and their circumstance. This suggests a tone that is controlled, or restrained, as very little is explicitly provided. Hence, (D) is correct.

3. D
Difficulty: Medium

Category: Reading / Command of Evidence

Strategic Advice: Use your thought process for answering the previous question to select the best piece of supporting information.

Getting to the Answer: In the previous question, you determined that the tone of the passage is best described as "restrained." As the narrator describes his father's lack of response to the news, the narrator also displays very little emotion toward this new development, never expressing his own feelings or opinions about the events that are unfolding. Thus, (D) provides the best support for the restrained tone found in the passage.

4. A
Difficulty: Medium

Category: Reading / Inference

Strategic Advice: When answer choices contain two words, make sure both words accurately answer the question stem.

Getting to the Answer: The interaction portrayed as the narrator enters his father's room conveys a hesitant nervousness that also reflects a kind of reverence, or awe, for his father. Though the narrator might project a slight wistfulness as he enters his father's room, there is no suggestion of outright disappointment, so C is incorrect. Choice (A) is correct.

5. A

Difficulty: Medium

Category: Reading / Command of Evidence

Strategic Advice: Working carefully on the previous question will reduce the amount of work required for Command of Evidence questions.

Getting to the Answer: When the narrator sees his father "glance disapprovingly at the lamp" (lines 15-16), he quickly lowers the wick so as not to displease his father. This instant response to his father's glance, along with his description of his father as having "still awesome features" (line 20), makes (A) the correct answer.

6. C

Difficulty: Medium

Category: Reading / Detail

Strategic Advice: The answers to most detail questions are stated explicitly in the passage. Avoid making inferences as you hone in on the correct answer.

Getting to the Answer: The first sentence of the passage reveals that the narrator hasn't been in the room in quite a while, and is momentarily taken aback. Though the last line of the passage implies that the father might be a large man (lines 73-75), A does not explain why the narrator is surprised by his father's room. Likewise, B is complete speculation, and D gives a detail never mentioned in the passage. Choice (C) is correct.

7. C

Difficulty: Medium

Category: Reading / Vocab-in-Context

Strategic Advice: Remember that although most of the answer choices are synonyms for the cited word in a Vocab-in-Context question, only one of them will appropriately fit in the context of the sentence.

Getting to the Answer: In the sentence, the narrator says that his father was hunched over either because of an infirmity or because he was in the habit of making room for the sloping ceilings. The father was modifying his behavior to account for, or adjust to, the odd ceilings. Choice (C) is correct.

8. D

Difficulty: Medium

Category: Reading / Vocab-in-Context

Strategic Advice: Do not be distracted by answer choices that appear more sophisticated than others.

Getting to the Answer: Use the phrase in which "relate" first appears ("to relate something to you") to your advantage. One cannot "connect something to you" without a set of physical changes (e.g., connecting wires to a robot), so eliminate B. Similarly, one might "associate something *with* you" (like a smell), but could not "associate something *to* you," so A is incorrect as well. In the context of the sentence, the narrator has come to "tell" his father something. Therefore, (D) is correct.

9. C

Difficulty: Hard

Category: Reading / Rhetoric

Strategic Advice: When you see the phrase "serves to" in a question stem, you are being asked to determine *why* the author or narrator of a passage does something.

Getting to the Answer: Though the narrator has tremendous respect for his father, as noted in B, the narrator's use of the third person in addressing his father has more to do with the intense formality, rigidity, and coldness of the relationship. Therefore, (C) is correct.

10. B

Difficulty: Medium

Category: Reading / Detail

Strategic Advice: Be careful when answering Detail questions that accompany a U.S. and World Literature passage; you are being asked to identify how a character acts, not how you think he might feel.

Getting to the Answer: After reading this passage and answering the previous questions, you've likely begun to notice a theme—the characters lack emotional development. Based on the behavior described, (B) is correct. The narrator's father is emotionless upon receiving news of his demotion. Although one can imagine that the father's lack of emotion might be the result of pride, as stated in C, the question is not asking you to interpret the father's underlying feelings or motivations. If you're tempted to select an answer choice to a Detail question based on a character's possible motivations, you're almost certainly going beyond what is written in the passage.

READING PRACTICE SET 7

Questions 1-11 are based on the following passages.

The following two passages discuss closely linked periods in European history. In Passage 1, the author describes the organization of the guild, an important feature of town life in medieval Europe. The author of Passage 2 identifies a fundamental social change that began taking place in Italian towns in the late 1200s.

Passage 1

The membership of guilds in medieval European towns was made up of masters, journeymen, and apprentices. Each guild differed from town to town
Line in its social and political influence, but its primary
5 economic function was the same everywhere—to protect the merchant and artisan, not just from the competition of foreign merchants, but also from the competition of fellow guild members. Town markets were closed to foreign products, and individual
10 members were prevented from growing rich at the expense of others.

Each guild adopted strict rules, including fixed hours of work, fixed prices and wages, limits on the numbers of workers in workshops, and regular
15 workshop inspections. These tightly enforced rules dampened personal ambition and initiative. No one was allowed to employ methods of production that were cheaper or more efficient than those used by fellow guild members. In fact, technical prog-
20 ress and those who favored it were looked on with suspicion.

Each local guild was organized hierarchically. The dominant members were the masters—small merchant proprietors of workshops who owned
25 their tools, raw materials, products, and all the profits from the sale of those products. Journeymen were wage-earning workers who had completed an apprenticeship. Apprentices were brought into a trade under a master's direction. The number of
30 masters in each local guild was limited, determined by the needs of the local market and by certain requirements, including citizenship, that were hard to fulfill.

The master functioned as a small, independent
35 entrepreneur whose primary capital included a house, a workshop, tools, and equipment. The number of workshop employees was restricted, usually to one or two apprentices and journeymen. If a master happened to inherit or marry into a fortune,
40 it could not be used against other masters, because the guild system left no room for competition. But material inequality among guild merchants was rare. For most of them, the economic structure of the guild meant the same kind of existence and the
45 same measured resources. While it gave them a secure position, it also prevented them from rising above it. In this sense, the guild system might be described as non-capitalist.

Passage 2

Throughout most of Europe in the late Middle
50 Ages, human consciousness as we know it today was really only half awake. People thought of themselves as members of a family, organization, or community, but not as individuals. In most countries, the different classes of society lived apart, each
55 with its own sense of values. Throughout their lives, people tended to remain in the class into which they were born. But in Italy social fluidity appeared early. By the late 1200s, Italy was brimming with the notion of individuality. The Italians of the next
60 two centuries—the period that we now call the Renaissance—were unafraid of being and appearing different from their neighbors.

Italian towns, primarily because of their control of Mediterranean trade, were the busiest in Europe.
65 Town crafts included such sophisticated trades as goldsmithing and stone carving. Competition between artisans grew so acute that masterpieces began to proliferate, and the love of art spread

throughout society. A few merchants made great
70 fortunes, lent their money to foreign princes, and
thus became international bankers.

Italy was a place in which the potential for
individual achievement—for a privileged few,
anyway—seemed unlimited. Because there was no
75 central Italian government, wealthy merchants were
unchecked in their political and social ambitions.
They competed for civic power and fame, spon-
sored public works and cultural institutions, hired
armies, and forged alliances. The typical Italian
80 merchant was fluent in Latin and Greek and read
the classic works of Rome and Greece. It was in
these circles that private, secular education got its
start.

The story of the Medici family of Florence illus-
85 trates these changes. Giovanni, an obscure merchant born in 1360, created the family banking fortune. His son Cosimo became ruler of Florence by
scheming against rivals in other Florentine families.
Cosimo's grandson and heir, Lorenzo the Magnifi-
90 cent, was an able politician, a famous patron of the
arts and learning, and a reputable scholar and poet.
The Medici family's rise to prominence coincided
with the decline of the guild and the growth of
capitalist individualism in Italy.

1. According to the author of Passage 1,
   the guilds created an economic system
   that was

   A) open and permissive.

   B) restrictive and stable.

   C) fluid and unpredictable.

   D) innovative and energetic.

2. Which choice provides the best evidence
   for the answer to the previous question?

   A) Lines 3-8 ("Each guild … guild
      members")

   B) Lines 29-30 ("The number …
      limited")

   C) Lines 43-47 ("For most … above it")

   D) Lines 66-71 ("Competition …
      international bankers")

3. As used in line 45, "measured" most
   nearly means

   A) deliberate.

   B) rhythmical.

   C) cautious.

   D) limited.

4. The author of Passage 2 describes human
   consciousness in most of Europe as being
   "only half awake" in line 51 to

   A) offer a generalization about prevail-
      ing social conditions in Europe in
      contrast to those in Italy.

   B) criticize a lack of interest in educa-
      tion in medieval European society.

   C) imply that some people have always
      opposed social progress.

   D) stress the role of individuality in
      contemporary society.

5. The author of Passage 2 uses the term
   "social fluidity" in line 57 primarily to
   describe the

   A) intense competition between families
      in Italian towns.

   B) great disparities of wealth among
      social classes in Italy.

   C) rapid spread of democratic institu-
      tions in Italy.

   D) unfixed character of social classes in
      Italy.

6. Which choice provides the best evidence for the answer to the previous question?

   A) Lines 51-53 ("People thought … as individuals")

   B) Lines 55-57 ("Throughout their … were born")

   C) Lines 58-59 ("By the late … individuality")

   D) Lines 59-62 ("The Italians … their neighbors")

7. According to Passage 2, much of Italy's success as a center of trade was due to its

   A) trade merchants' fluency in Latin and Greek.

   B) talented goldsmiths and stone carvers.

   C) control of trade around the Mediterranean Sea.

   D) lack of central government.

8. As used in line 67, "acute" most nearly means

   A) chaotic.

   B) dangerous.

   C) keen.

   D) sudden.

9. Both passages seek to explain the

   A) expanding role of commerce in Italian towns during the Middle Ages.

   B) economic structure of the guild system during the Middle Ages.

   C) fast growth of capitalism during the Middle Ages.

   D) circumstances of merchants during the Middle Ages.

10. The merchants discussed in Passage 1 are most different from those discussed in Passage 2 in their

    A) attitudes regarding personal ambition.

    B) interest in exercising their rights as citizens.

    C) views regarding the right to own private property.

    D) concern for the economic welfare of their towns.

11. What position would the author of Passage 1 most likely take regarding the description of European society in lines 53-57?

    A) The structure of the medieval guild and its effects could be said to support the description.

    B) The description underestimates the extent to which the medieval guild system favored individual initiative.

    C) The accuracy of the description cannot be determined without further investigation.

    D) It is unwise to describe European society in such sweeping terms.

ANSWERS & EXPLANATIONS

1. B

2. C

3. D

4. A

5. D

6. B

7. C

8. C

9. D

10. A

11. A

1. B
Difficulty: Medium

Category: Reading / Detail

Strategic Advice: Read Paired Passages and answer their questions separately so you do not select answer choices that refer to the other passage.

Getting to the Answer: The author writes at great length of the restrictions the system placed on the guilds. However, at the same time that these restrictions prevented guild members from improving on their position, they also ensured that those positions would be secure. Therefore, (B) is correct.

2. C
Difficulty: Medium

Category: Reading / Command of Evidence

Strategic Advice: The correct answer to the previous question includes two descriptive words. Therefore, the correct answer to this question must provide support for both descriptions, not just one.

Getting to the Answer: Answers A and C are incorrect, as they each support only one of the descriptive words in the correct answer to the previous question. Choice D is incorrect, as it occurs in Passage 2. Choice (C) is correct because by being selective in their membership, the guilds were restrictive but offered security to their members.

3. D
Difficulty: Medium

Category: Reading / Vocab-in-Context

Strategic Advice: Determine which answer choice makes the most sense in the context of the paragraph's intended meaning.

Getting to the Answer: In the fourth paragraph of Passage 1, "measured" is describing the limited resources available to guild merchants. Though A, B, and C are synonyms of "measured," none of them fit in this context. Therefore, (D), "limited," is correct because it best captures the meaning that there were not enough resources.

4. A
Difficulty: Hard

Category: Reading / Rhetoric

Strategic Advice: Notice that even though the question stem refers to a specific line number, you must consider content from the entirety of the first paragraph of Passage 2 to correctly answer the question.

Getting to the Answer: The author wants to make a generalization about what was happening in most of Europe, which helps set up a contrast with the new developments in Italy. In the passage, the author isn't praising or condemning; he or she is just describing. Watch out for out-of-scope answer choices. Choice B brings up the topic of education, which isn't discussed until the end of the third paragraph, and though D mentions the idea of individuality, the author is not interested in modern society. Choice (A) is correct.

5. D
Difficulty: Medium

Category: Reading / Rhetoric

Strategic Advice: Whenever a question asks why an author has chosen to use a particular term, carefully examine the paragraph in which it appears.

Getting to the Answer: By using the term "social fluidity," the author is able to convey the flexible, or "fluid," nature of Italy's social classes, as opposed to the fixed, rigid nature of the social class system in the majority of Europe at the time. In Italy, it was possible to move among social classes, rather than being locked into the class of one's birth status. Choice (D) provides the best match for this idea and is therefore correct.

6. B
Difficulty: Medium

Category: Reading / Command of Evidence

Strategic Advice: Use your work in answering the previous question to help you select the correct answer choice.

Getting to the Answer: All of the answer choices fall in the same paragraph as the term "social fluidity," but you need to select the answer choice that emphasizes motion through the classes. Only (B) provides direct evidence that, in contrast to the rest of Europe, Italy experienced "social fluidity," or the ability for someone to transition beyond the class they were born into. Choice (B) is correct.

7. C
Difficulty: Medium

Category: Reading / Detail

Strategic Advice: This question involves details only from Passage 2. Trap answer choices may involve information from Passage 1 and will therefore be out of scope.

Getting to the Answer: In the second paragraph of Passage 2, the author states that Italian towns "were the busiest in Europe" (line 64) "primarily because of their control of Mediterranean trade" (lines 63-64). Therefore, (C) is correct; it is the only answer choice that describes how the country became a successful *center*, or focal point, of trade.

8. C
Difficulty: Medium

Category: Reading / Vocab-in-Context

Strategic Advice: Eliminate any answer choices that skew the intended meaning of the sentence.

Getting to the Answer: According to the passage, competition among the artists was intense. There isn't evidence to suggest it was chaotic or dangerous, and you don't know if the competition arose suddenly or gradually. Only (C), "keen" is a match for intense, and is therefore correct.

9. D
Difficulty: Medium

Category: Reading / Synthesis

Strategic Advice: Use your Passage Map to determine what purpose both passages share. Eliminate answer choices that pertain to only one of the passages.

Getting to the Answer: When there isn't a lot of overlap between paired passages, you'll have to consider the broader ideas to find points of agreement. Both passages describe trade during the Middle Ages, specifically the role of merchants. This is a great match for (D), which is the correct answer.

10. A

Difficulty: Medium

Category: Reading / Synthesis

Strategic Advice: Use your Passage Map to summarize and compare the role of merchants in each passage.

Getting to the Answer: The merchants mentioned in Passage 1 were working within the closed system of the guild, which had numerous restrictions that actually discouraged individual initiative. On the other hand, the merchants in Passage 2 "were unchecked in their political and social ambitions" (lines 75-76). Thus, the personal ambitions of these two groups of merchants were radically different, making (A) correct.

11. A

Category: Reading / Synthesis

Difficulty: Hard

Strategic Advice: Before selecting an answer choice, think carefully about the attitude, or tone, that the author of Passage 1 conveys toward the topic.

Getting to the Answer: Though the author of Passage 1 is fairly objective in his or her description of the medieval guild system, various phrases, such as "dampening personal ambition" (line 16), "technical progress and those who favored it were looked on with suspicion" (lines 19-21), and "prevented them from rising above it" (lines 19-21), suggest a slightly negative attitude toward the restrictiveness of the

guilds. Therefore, the author of Passage 1 would most likely take the position that the structure of the medieval guild and its effects supports the idea expressed in lines 53-57. This matches (A), which is correct.

READING PRACTICE SET 8

Questions 1-11 are based on the following passages.

Passage 1 discusses how surgeons might be able to use a bone-inducing protein found in cows to help patients. Passage 2 explores the advances made in developing artificial organs and using them in surgical procedures.

Passage 1

Surgeons can perform phenomenal feats. They replace clogged coronary arteries with blood vessels from the leg. They reconnect capillaries, tendons, and nerves to reattach severed fingers. They even
5 refashion parts of intestines to create new bladders. But surgeons find it difficult to reconstruct complicated bones like the jawbone or those of the inner ear. And only rarely can they replace large bones lost to disease or injury.
10 The challenge stems from the nature of bones. Unlike other types of tissue, bones with one normal shape cannot be reworked into other shapes. Nor can doctors move large bones from one part of the body to another without severely disabling a
15 person. Existing treatments for bone defects are all short-term and limited. Surgeons can replace some diseased joints with plastic or metal implants, but artificial hips or knees steadily loosen and must be reconstructed every few years.
20 Fortunately, surgeons are beginning to overcome these obstacles by creating bone substitutes from, of all things, muscle. The idea of making bones from muscle is not all that strange. Muscle, bone, fat, blood vessels, and bone marrow all develop in
25 human embryos from the same loosely organized tissue.
In 1987 scientists isolated a bone-inducing protein called osteogenin from cows. Osteogenin can make undifferentiated human tissue produce
30 cartilage and bone. But few surgeons have used osteogenin because it is hard to control. If sprinkled
directly onto a defect, for instance, the entire area might stiffen to bone if a tiny bit fell on surrounding blood vessels and nerves.
35 More recently, plastic surgeons have circumvented that snag by prefabricating bones away from the immediate site of a defect. Flaps of animal thigh muscles are taken and placed in osteogenin-coated silicone-rubber molds of the desired shape. The
40 molds are implanted in the same animal's abdomen to provide a suitable biologic environment for transforming muscle into bone. Within weeks, the molds yield tiny, perfectly detailed bone segments.
So far, surgeons have made bones from muscles
45 in small animals but have not yet tried the process in humans. For one thing, osteogenin is available only in small amounts. Secondly, the safety and effectiveness of the process must first be tested on larger animals.

Passage 2

50 We have entered a new era in medicine. In scarcely more than a generation, artificial organs have evolved from temporary substitutes to long-functioning devices. Millions of people live with cardiac pacemakers, arterial grafts, hip-joint pros-
55 theses, middle-ear implants, and intraocular lenses. Eventually, artificial organs will allow ordinary, healthy people to live longer—or, more appropriately, to die young at a ripe age. So far, though, even the best substitutes lag far behind their natural
60 counterparts. But the obstacles to better implants are not purely technical. Because such devices require human testing, their development poses a challenge to our cultural and ethical values.
Although many patients volunteer for tests of
65 unproven medical devices, such altruism—and the medical progress it engenders—is hampered by medical ethicists and others who call for more restrictions on human testing. While people favoring restrictions are well-intentioned, their standards
70 are inappropriate.

The only way to gain the information needed for refining artificial organs is through experiments on people. Research using animals will not suffice. The mechanics of bone joints, for example, differ
75 markedly from species to species. The replacement of wrists, knees, and finger joints poses complex engineering problems because of the heavy mechanical loads involved and the range of motion required. Because there is no generally accepted
80 large-animal model for the human bones and joints that orthopedic devices are designed to replace, human evaluation is essential.

In developing each new implant, the experience gained from human testing becomes the critical
85 bottleneck in the experimental process. In the case of artificial heart devices, engineering design is not currently the main obstacle. Heart implants can sustain patients for weeks while they await transplants. These results are achieved with a variety of
90 devices. But in other cases, the same devices can fail to keep patients alive. It appears that success depends less on the particular model used than on the patient's age, overall health, and the quality of postoperative care.
95 Clearly, what is lacking today in coronary care is not new devices or techniques but simply more experience. How much blood should be pumped, and for how long? How can the natural heart be weaned from mechanical assistance? When do
100 the risks outweigh the benefits of further surgical assistance? There is little justification for developing new designs until such questions are adequately answered, and they can be answered only in human subjects.

1. The tone of Passage 1 suggests that the text might appear in
   A) an introductory science textbook.
   B) a feature article in a popular science magazine.
   C) an academic paper for doctors.
   D) an editorial in a major newspaper.

2. According to Passage 1, why has muscle been successfully used in creating bone substitutes?
   A) Bones can't be relocated from one part of the body to another.
   B) Muscle resembles cartilage, which is a soft form of bone.
   C) Muscles can be retrained to function in place of diseased or injured bones.
   D) Bone and muscle both develop from the same tissue in human embryos.

3. As used in line 37, "immediate" most nearly means
   A) nearby.
   B) instant.
   C) next in line.
   D) directly understood.

4. Passage 2 most clearly implies that
   A) animal research often leads to questions of ethics.
   B) humans by nature enjoy contributing to medical advances that benefit society.
   C) animal research can only benefit humans to a certain extent.
   D) humans are more advanced in their physiological development than other animals.

5. Which choice provides the best evidence for the answer to the previous question?
   A) Lines 64-68 ("Although many … human testing")
   B) Line 73 ("Research … not suffice")
   C) Lines 79-82 ("Because there is … evaluation is essential")
   D) Lines 83-85 ("In developing each … experimental process")

6. The author of passage 2 uses the phrase "to die young at a ripe age" in line 58 to convey

   A) dying young of an illness prevalent among older people.

   B) extending one's life despite being ill.

   C) living much longer than the average life span.

   D) maintaining a healthier body into old age.

7. As used in line 84, "critical" most nearly means

   A) skeptical.

   B) significant.

   C) fault-finding.

   D) perceptive.

8. Which of the following best describes the central purpose of each passage?

   A) Passage 1 informs readers about new medical developments, while Passage 2 tries to convince readers that testing restrictions are hampering medical progress.

   B) Passage 1 commends the latest medical feats, while Passage 2 criticizes medical research.

   C) Both passages serve the purpose of praising new medical advances.

   D) Both passages serve the purpose of showing the limitations of medical research.

9. The author of Passage 2 would most likely respond to the statement in lines 47-48 that "the safety and effectiveness" of using artificial bones must first be tested on large animals before the process is tried on humans by

   A) applauding the precaution suggested by the statement.

   B) saying that it's time to begin human testing.

   C) suggesting it depends on which large animals were used in the testing.

   D) proposing that surgeons receive better training in the use of osteogenin.

10. Which choice provides the best evidence for the answer to the previous question?

   A) Lines 53-55 ("Millions of … lenses")

   B) Lines 58-60 ("So far … counterparts")

   C) Lines 71-73 ("The only way … on people")

   D) Lines 101-104 ("There is … in human subjects")

11. The last paragraph of Passage 2 is similar to the last paragraph of Passage 1 in its emphasis on the need to

   A) develop new and improved devices for human implantation.

   B) focus primarily on medical experiments with larger animals.

   C) proceed immediately to medical experiments using humans.

   D) gather information that is relevant to the treatment of human patients.

ANSWERS & EXPLANATIONS

1. B
2. D
3. A
4. C
5. C
6. D
7. B
8. A
9. B
10. C
11. D

1. B
Difficulty: Medium

Category: Reading / Rhetoric

Strategic Advice: Think about the words, phrases, and sentence structures the author uses, as well as the information presented, in order to determine the intended audience.

Getting to the Answer: The language used and information presented in Passage 1 seem too difficult to appear in an introductory science textbook, so eliminate A. Similarly, the language and information do not reflect the level of sophistication one would expect in an academic paper for doctors who already have a good deal of medical knowledge, so C is incorrect as well. Choice D may be tempting because newspaper articles are often informative in tone, a newspaper editorial offers an opinion, so D is incorrect. Instead, the tone suggests that the passage is intended for people who are interested in the topic but are not medical professionals—a great match for (B).

2. D
Difficulty: Medium

Category: Reading / Detail

Strategic Advice: Use your Passage Map to locate the part of the passage that discusses the topic mentioned in the question stem.

Getting to the Answer: Be careful—don't let your own opinions become a part of your reasoning process. The third paragraph states that "Muscle, bone, fat, blood vessels, and bone marrow all develop in human embryos from the same loosely organized tissue" (lines 23-26). This has allowed scientists to make use of the shared tissue properties of bone and muscle, thus creating bone substitutes out of muscle; therefore, (D) is the correct answer.

3. A
Difficulty: Medium

Category: Reading / Vocab-in-Context

Strategic Advice: Eliminate answer choices that do not make sense in the context of the sentence.

Getting to the Answer: In the sentence in which the word "immediate" appears, the author is contrasting a new process with an old one. Surgeons used to use osteogenin at the site of a defect, which led to a problem controlling the substance. In stating that the new process involves placing the bone away from the "immediate site of the defect" (line 37), it is clear that "immediate" means "nearby." Therefore, (A) is correct.

4. C
Difficulty: Medium

Category: Reading / Inference

Strategic Advice: When a question requires you to make an inference, remember that the answer is not stated explicitly in the passage. Instead, you must draw conclusions based on the information provided.

Getting to the Answer: The main reason that the author of Passage 2 thinks human testing is required is because animal research cannot thoroughly replicate the conditions that exist in humans. Therefore, it can be reasonably inferred from the passage that the author thinks animal research can only benefit humans to a certain extent, making (C) the correct answer.

5. C
Difficulty: Medium

Category: Reading / Command of Evidence

Strategic Advice: Eliminate answer choices that do not directly support the correct answer to the previous question.

Getting to the Answer: The correct answer to the previous question is that animal research can benefit humans only to a certain extent. Choice (C) supports this logical inference by pointing out a major drawback in animal testing—that there is no large-animal model that exists for human bones and joints. Hence, the view that animal testing can only help humans to a certain extent.

6. D
Difficulty: Hard

Category: Reading / Rhetoric

Strategic Advice: Study the context of the paragraph in order to understand what the author means by using the phrase in question.

Getting to the Answer: This question is tricky, so break the phrase down into pieces in order to make it more manageable. Dying at a "ripe age" means dying when old, while the author uses dying "young" to suggest still feeling

young as an elderly person. The phrase does not mean dying young of an old person's illness, as stated in A, nor does it mean extending one's life despite being ill, as stated in B. The author is discussing the eventual benefits of artificial organs: ordinary people can live longer, healthier lives, and can even die "young at a ripe age." This matches (D), which is the correct answer.

7. B
Difficulty: Medium

Category: Reading / Vocab-in-Context

Strategic Advice: Pretend the cited word is a blank in the sentence. Predict a word that could fill that blank, then select the answer choice that best matches your prediction.

Getting to the Answer: In this sentence, the author is saying that the need to use humans leads to a major bottleneck in the experimental process. Common uses of the word "critical" do not make sense in the context of the passage. Words like "skeptical," "fault-finding," and "perceptive" are common definitions of the word, but are not correct in this setting. Choice (B), "significant," is a great match and is the correct answer.

8. A
Difficulty: Hard

Category: Synthesis

Strategic Advice: Use your Passage Map to determine the central purpose each author has for sharing information with his or her readers.

Getting to the Answer: In Passage 1, the author conveys a good deal of information about the current status of bone replacement; his or her main purpose is to inform readers. In Passage 2, the author also conveys information; however, his or her main purpose is to convince readers to agree with the opinion that human testing restrictions limit medical progress. You can use the tone in each passage to help eliminate answer choices. Passage 1 is neutrally descriptive, not adulatory, so you can eliminate B and C. Since limitations of medical research are discussed only in Passage 2, you can eliminate D as well. Choice (A) is correct.

9. B
Difficulty: Hard

Category: Reading / Synthesis

Strategic Advice: Use your Passage Map to search Passage 2 for statements that indicate the author's stance on the topic cited in the question stem.

Getting to the Answer: Throughout Passage 2, the author expresses a desire for human testing to become a more acceptable—and direct—way of advancing medical progress for the sake of humanity. This is especially true, since he says there is no acceptable large-animal model for bones and joints. Therefore, the author of Passage 2 would probably disagree with the statement in Passage 1's last paragraph that larger animals must first be tested before the process is tested on humans. Choice (B) is correct.

10. C
Difficulty: Medium

Category: Reading / Command of Evidence

Strategic Advice: Use your work for the previous question to quickly answer a Command of Evidence follow-up question.

Getting to the Answer: Choices A and B are incorrect, as they occur early in the passage before the author has revealed much about his or her position. While D might seem correct in that it focuses on the need for human subjects, it is not the correct answer choice because the quotation occurs as the author specifically

discusses coronary care. Choice (C) is correct because it provides a general, direct statement of the author's strong position.

11. D
Difficulty: Hard

Category: Reading / Synthesis

Strategic Advice: Remember that the correct answer will reflect an idea that is implied in both paragraphs.

Getting to the Answer: The last paragraph of Passage 1 states that the process of bone prefabrication has not yet been tried on humans—that it needs to be tested on large animals first. The last paragraph of Passage 2 features questions about coronary care that can be answered only through human testing. In other words, both authors are stressing the need to gather information that's relevant to the treatment of human patients. Choice (D) is correct.

The Writing & Language Test

The Kaplan Method for Writing & Language

The Kaplan Method for Writing & Language is the method you will use to boost your score on the Writing & Language Test. By understanding what the question is looking for, how it relates to the passage, and what questions you should ask yourself on Test Day, you will maximize the number of points you earn. Use the Kaplan Method for Writing & Language for every SAT Writing & Language Test passage and question you encounter, whether practicing, completing your homework, working on a Practice Test, or taking the actual exam on Test Day.

The Kaplan Method for Writing & Language has three steps:

Step 1: Read the passage and identify the issue

- If there's an infographic, apply the Kaplan Method for Infographics.

Step 2: Eliminate answer choices that do not address the issue

Step 3: Plug in the remaining answer choices and select the most correct, concise, and relevant one

Step 1: Read the passage and identify the issue

This means:

- Rather than reading the whole passage and then answering all of the questions, you can answer questions as you read because they are mostly embedded in the text itself.

- When you see a number, stop reading and look at the question. If you can answer it with what you've read so far, do so. If you need more information, keep reading for context until you can answer the question.

Step 2: Eliminate answer choices that do not address the issue

Eliminating answer choices that do not address the issue:

- Increases your odds of getting the correct answer by removing obviously incorrect answer choices.

Step 3: Plug in the remaining answer choices and select the most correct, concise, and relevant one

Correct, concise, and relevant means that the answer choice you select:

- Makes sense when read with the correction

- Is as short as possible while retaining the information in the text

- Relates well to the passage overall

Answer choices should not:

- Change the intended meaning of the original sentence, paragraph, or passage

- Introduce new grammatical errors, even if the answer choice in question resolves the initial issue in the passage

WRITING & LANGUAGE PRACTICE SET 1

Questions 1-11 are based on the following passage and supplementary material.

Renewal and Reworking: Today's American Textile Industry

At its **1** top in the years following World War II, the American textile industry dominated both the national and global workplaces. However, by the 1990s, employment in the textile industry had plummeted from an all-time high of 1.3 million jobs to approximately 672,000. Even more alarming was that the numbers would keep **2** dropping—dramatically.

The reason for the decline was clear: The American government began allowing the outsourcing of jobs to foreign manufacturers, who promised cheap labor and production costs. The most notable example of this shift was the 1994 signing of NAFTA, or the North American Free Trade Agreement, which allowed inexpensive textile imports from Mexico. It also gave American textile companies an incentive to move production south where lower costs meant higher **3** profits, the entry of China into world markets as a major competitor with less expensive exports also contributed to a decline in the number of American textile manufacturing jobs. **4**

1. A) NO CHANGE
   B) height
   C) leap
   D) stature

2. A) NO CHANGE
   B) dropping. Dramatically
   C) dropping, dramatically
   D) dropping; dramatically

3. A) NO CHANGE
   B) profits the
   C) profits. The
   D) profits! The

4. Which sentence, if added at this point, best reflects the information presented in the graph?

   A) The number of textile and apparel jobs began to decline steadily in the 1970s.

   B) Textile and apparel jobs reached their peak in the 1950s after a steady increase.

   C) The number of textile manufacturing jobs remained relatively stable during the 1950s and 1960s.

   D) There was a sharp decline in textile and apparel jobs following the signing of NAFTA.

[1] But signs **5** <u>suggests</u> that amount of textile work in the United States is on the rise again. [2] In 2014, the industry employed 232,000 people, making up roughly 2 percent of the American workforce. [3] While that percentage is a far cry from that of the industry's heyday, it shows that textile manufacturers are re-evaluating business. [4] The textile industry produces the materials needed to make clothing, such as yarn and cotton. **6**

According to industry insiders, the United States is still a viable competitor in global textile manufacturing. Not only does the United States have the means to produce raw materials such as cotton and human-made fibers, but it also possesses a workforce that is becoming savvier in the global marketplace. Many American textile companies have turned inward and spent money on retooling manufacturing centers, studying work flow and costs, and looking for niche markets for **7** <u>exact</u> goods. Also, increased consumer concern has made environmentally safe products made in the United States preferable. **8**

5. A) NO CHANGE
   B) suggest
   C) suggested
   D) did suggest

6. Which sentence should be omitted to improve the focus of this paragraph?
   A) Sentence 1
   B) Sentence 2
   C) Sentence 3
   D) Sentence 4

7. A) NO CHANGE
   B) distinct
   C) particular
   D) unusual

8. Which sentence, if added at this point, would best support the paragraph's central idea?
   A) China continues to produce the largest amount of cotton in the world.
   B) China, India, and Germany continue to export more textiles than the United States.
   C) Not everyone is willing to pay more for garments made from textiles produced in the United States.
   D) Rising costs in overseas factories have also helped drive interest in bringing the industry back to America.

Technology plays a large role in the profits of American textile manufacturing. With new machinery and advanced systems, United States factories can be on the cutting edge of product design, ⑨ research; and development.

While much of this tentative increase is driven by the ups and downs of the economy, a trend of Americans feeling more optimistic about the future tends to lead to an increase in consumer spending. More dollars can help the American textile industry maintain ⑩ it's prominence in markets at home and abroad. Currently, the United States ⑪ ranking fourth in textile exports, behind only China, India, and Germany. With increased interest in retooling production at home, the American textile industry's future looks much brighter.

Textile and Apparel Jobs, 1940–2000

Y-axis: Textile and Apparel Employment (millions): 0, 0.5, 1.0, 1.5, 2.0, 2.5, 3.0

X-axis: Year: 1940, 1950, 1960, 1970, 1980, 1990, 2000

Source: USDA Economic Research Service estimates based on U.S. Department of Labor, Bureau of Labor Statistics, *Current Employment Statistics* survey.

9. A) NO CHANGE
   B) research and
   C) research, and
   D) research—and

10. A) NO CHANGE
    B) its
    C) their
    D) they're

11. A) NO CHANGE
    B) rank
    C) ranks
    D) will rank

ANSWERS & EXPLANATIONS

1. B
2. A
3. C
4. D
5. B
6. D
7. C
8. D
9. C
10. B
11. C

1. B
Difficulty: Medium

Category: Writing & Language / Effective Language Use

Strategic Advice: Reread each answer choice into the sentence to determine which word best expresses the author's central idea.

Getting to the Answer: In this context, the author is trying to convey that the textile industry was at its highest point in the years following World War II. While "top" could convey this, the phrase "at its top" sounds awkward, making A incorrect. Neither C nor D makes sense in context, so they are also incorrect. Choice (B), "height," is correct.

2. A
Difficulty: Medium

Category: Writing & Language / Punctuation

Strategic Advice: When a dash is included in an underlined segment, determine what its purpose is.

Getting to the Answer: In this sentence, the dash is used correctly to emphasize a modifier ("dramatically"). Choices B, C, and D are incorrect because they introduce sentence formation errors. Choice (A) is therefore correct because no change is needed.

3. C
Difficulty: Easy

Category: Writing & Language / Sentence Formation

Strategic Advice: First, determine whether the ideas expressed should be linked or divided. Then, select the answer choices that features a punctuation mark that does so without introducing a new error.

Getting to the Answer: As written, this sentence contains two independent clauses joined by a comma, also known as a run-on sentence. A period is needed to separate these independent clauses into two distinct sentences. Choice (C) is correct.

4. D
Difficulty: Hard

Category: Writing & Language / Quantitative

Strategic Advice: The correct answer choice will not only reflect the information in the graph, but also support the central idea of the paragraph.

Getting to the Answer: This paragraph is primarily about the reasons behind the decline in the number of textile jobs in the United States. The author provides the signing of NAFTA as one of the reasons behind this decline. Choice (D) is correct because it supports the central idea of the paragraph and correctly reflects the information presented in the graph.

5. B

Difficulty: Easy

Category: Writing & Language / Usage

Strategic Advice: When a sole verb is underlined, determine what its subject is and whether it agrees with its subject in person and number.

Getting to the Answer: The subject of this sentence is "signs," which is plural. The underlined verb "suggests," however, is singular and therefore incorrect. Choice (B) is correct because it fixes the error with the plural "suggest."

6. D

Difficulty: Medium

Category: Writing & Language / Development

Strategic Advice: Identify the paragraph's central idea. Select the answer choice that does not directly relate to the central idea.

Getting to the Answer: The central idea of this paragraph is the rise of the amount of textile work in the United States. Choice (D) is correct because while sentence 4 contains details relevant to the passage's overall topic, it does not contribute to the central idea of this particular paragraph.

7. C

Difficulty: Hard

Category: Writing & Language / Effective Language Use

Strategic Advice: Read each answer choice into the sentence in place of the underlined word to determine which answer choice best captures the sentence's central idea.

Getting to the Answer: A "niche" market is a specific segment of a broader industry (in this case, textile manufacturing). In this context, "particular" (meaning "specific") best describes

the goods that are chosen for a niche market. Choice (C) is correct.

8. D

Difficulty: Hard

Category: Writing & Language / Development

Strategic Advice: Identify the paragraph's central idea and determine which answer choice contains details that support that idea.

Getting to the Answer: In this paragraph, the author claims that the United States is still a competitor in the global textile manufacturing industry. Choice (D) is correct because it provides details about why American textile companies are turning inward, thus supporting the paragraph's central claim.

9. C

Difficulty: Medium

Category: Writing & Language / Punctuation

Strategic Advice: On the SAT, items in a series of three or more elements need to be separated by commas.

Getting to the Answer: The underlined portion of the sentence is part of a series of three items: product design, research, and development. A comma is needed after "research" and before "and" to denote the next and last item in the series. Choice (C) is correct.

10. B

Difficulty: Hard

Category: Writing & Language / Usage

Strategic Advice: Confirm that the correct part of speech is being used and that any underlined pronouns agree with their respective antecedents.

Getting to the Answer: The underlined "it's" is a contraction for "it is" or "it was," which does not make sense in context. Choice C is incorrect because "their" is the possessive form of the third person pronoun "they," which does not agree with the singular antecedent ("the American textile industry"). Choice D is incorrect because "they're" is a contraction for "they are" or "they were." The underlined word should be the singular possessive pronoun "its." Choice (B) is correct.

11. C

Difficulty: Medium

Category: Writing & Language / Usage

Strategic Advice: When a verb is underlined, determine its subject and whether that subject is singular or plural. If you can't identify the issue when a verb is underlined, look for clues in the sentence that might indicate that another tense or number should be used.

Getting to the Answer: As written, the underlined portion creates a fragment because of its gerund form (*–ing*). The use of "currently" at the beginning of the sentence indicates the verb should be present tense, so eliminate D, which is in the future tense. The subject of this sentence is "United States," which is singular, so eliminate B, which is plural. Choice (C) is therefore correct.

WRITING & LANGUAGE PRACTICE SET 2

Questions 1-11 are based on the following passage.

The Human Heart

The heart is responsible for moving blood to all of the body's tissues through a 60,000-mile network of vessels. The pumping of the heart relies on ❶ a convoluted system of muscle (myocardium), valves, coronary vessels, the conduction (electrical) system, ❷ arteries and veins—and the sac around the heart (pericardium).

[1] The human heart is divided into four chambers, the walls of which are made of the myocardium, the muscle that contracts rhythmically under the ❸ stimulation of electrical currents. [2] The heart is able to pump blood in a coordinated manner because of the arrangement of the cells and the electrical messages that pass easily between the cells. [3] This cardiovascular pump operates by squeezing blood out of its chambers (contraction) and then expanding to allow blood in (relaxation). [4] The action is similar to squeezing water out of a soft plastic bottle while holding it underwater and then releasing one's grasp so that water is sucked back into the bottle as it re-expands. [5] The myocardium is composed of individual muscle cells called myocytes, which work together to contract and relax the heart chambers in the correct sequence to pump blood to the lungs and the body. ▮4

The right side of the ❺ heart, which is composed of the

1. A) NO CHANGE
    B) a puzzling
    C) an involved
    D) an intricate

2. A) NO CHANGE
    B) arteries and veins and
    C) arteries and veins, and
    D) arteries and veins; and

3. A) NO CHANGE
    B) invigoration
    C) excitation
    D) determination

4. To make this paragraph most logical, sentence 5 should be placed

    A) where it is now.
    B) after sentence 1.
    C) after sentence 2.
    D) after sentence 3.

5. A) NO CHANGE
    B) heart, which is composed of the right atrium and right ventricle, is
    C) heart; which is composed of the right atrium and right ventricle, is
    D) heart which is composed of the right atrium and right ventricle is

right atrium and right ventricle is responsible for pulmonary circulation. That is, it pumps blood through the lungs, where **6** they receive oxygen and rids itself of carbon dioxide. The left side of the heart, composed of the left atrium and left ventricle, receives the newly oxygenated **7** blood, it pumps it through the body where it delivers oxygen and picks up carbon dioxide (waste). Blood must circle from the right side of the heart and through the lungs before being delivered to the left side and throughout the body.

"Used blood" returns to the right side of the heart via **8** two large veins. The superior vena cava (from the head and arms) and the inferior vena cava (from the legs and abdomen). Blood from the right heart is dark bluish red because it is deoxygenated, or lacks oxygen. The blood from the left heart is oxygenated and therefore is bright red. Blood from the left heart is delivered to the body through the aorta, the largest blood vessel in the body.

9 Indeed the heart never rests while it supplies blood to the rest of the body, it actually works harder than any other

6. A) NO CHANGE
   B) it receives
   C) one receives
   D) some receive

7. A) NO CHANGE
   B) blood it pumps
   C) blood, and pumps
   D) blood and pumps

8. A) NO CHANGE
   B) two large veins the superior vena cava
   C) two large veins, the superior vena cava
   D) two large veins; the superior vena cava

9. A) NO CHANGE
   B) Because
   C) Whenever
   D) While

muscle in the body and needs a much richer blood supply than other muscles. Although the heart makes up less than 1 percent of a person's body weight, it requires 4 to 5 percent of **10** its blood. **11**

10. A) NO CHANGE
    B) it's
    C) the body's
    D) the bodies

11. Which answer choice most effectively establishes the central idea of the passage?

    A) The heart is responsible for moving blood to all of the body's tissues through a 60,000-mile network of vessels.

    B) Scientists are conducting cutting-edge research regarding how the heart pumps blood through the body.

    C) The heart is thought by some to be the seat of the soul, though others view it in purely clinical terms.

    D) The heart oxygenates the body by moving blood to all of the body's tissues.

ANSWERS & EXPLANATIONS

1. D

2. C

3. A

4. B

5. B

6. B

7. D

8. C

9. B

10. C

11. A

1. D
Difficulty: Medium

Category: Writing & Language / Effective Language Use

Strategic Advice: Do not answer a question until you have read enough information to do so.

Getting to the Answer: The first two paragraphs describe how the heart pumps blood. The system is made up of many interconnected parts, making it "complicated," or "intricate." Choice (D) is correct.

2. C
Difficulty: Medium

Category: Writing & Language / Punctuation

Strategic Advice: If an underlined segment contains elements in a series, determine if the correct punctuation is used to separate the items from one another.

Getting to the Answer: This sentence contains a series of distinct elements: muscle (myocardium),

valves, coronary vessels, the conduction (electrical) system, arteries and veins, and the sac around the heart (pericardium). Commas are required to separate each element in the series, including the element before "and." Choice (C) is correct.

3. A
Difficulty: Medium

Category: Writing & Language / Effective Language Use

Strategic Advice: Reread the sentence in which the underlined word appears. Predict a word that describes the action of the electrical currents. Then, determine which answer choice is the closest match to your prediction.

Getting to the Answer: The electrical currents act in a way that causes the myocardium to contract rhythmically. The word that describes this action most precisely is "stimulation," so the underlined segment is correct as written. Choice (A) is correct.

4. B
Difficulty: Hard

Category: Writing & Language / Organization

Strategic Advice: Reread sentence 5 in the context of the entire paragraph to determine its logical placement.

Getting to the Answer: Sentence 5 provides additional details about the myocardium. It most logically belongs after sentence 1, in which "myocardium" is initially defined. Choice (B) is correct.

5. B

Difficulty: Medium

Category: Writing & Language / Punctuation

Strategic Advice: Determine the relationship of the underlined portion to the rest of the sentence. If it does not provide information essential to the intended meaning, punctuation is required to separate it from the sentence's central idea.

Getting to the Answer: The subordinate clause "which is composed of the right atrium and right ventricle" is not essential to understanding the meaning of the sentence. Therefore, it should be enclosed by commas. Choice (B) is correct.

6. B

Difficulty: Easy

Category: Writing & Language / Usage

Strategic Advice: Be sure to correctly identify an underlined pronoun's antecedent and whether it is singular or plural. You may need to read the previous sentence to determine the antecedent.

Getting to the Answer: The pronoun refers to "blood," which is singular, so the underlined segment is incorrect as written. The pronouns used to refer to the same antecedent in other parts of the sentence are "it" and "itself." Choice (B) uses "it," maintaining pronoun agreement, and is correct.

7. D

Difficulty: Medium

Category: Writing & Language / Sentence Formation

Strategic Advice: Determine how the parts of the sentence on either side of the comma after "blood" are related and how those parts can be combined to best convey that relationship.

Getting to the Answer: The second half of the sentence is part of a compound predicate that follows the subject, "the left side of the heart." The two predicates that make up the compound predicate are "receives the newly oxygenated blood" and "pumps it through the body." No punctuation is needed to join the parts of a compound predicate. Choice (D) is correct.

8. C

Difficulty: Medium

Category: Writing & Language / Sentence Formation

Strategic Advice: Identify whether the two sentences on either side of the period are, in fact, complete sentences. If they are not, select the answer choice that correctly combines the two parts.

Getting to the Answer: The second "sentence" is not really a sentence—it's a fragment that describes the "two large veins" mentioned in the previous sentence. The fragment should be joined to the previous sentence with a comma. Choice (C) is correct.

9. B

Difficulty: Medium

Category: Writing & Language / Organization

Strategic Advice: Read the passage before and after the underlined word. Think about the relationship between the two sentences, as well as the relationship between the parts of the sentence that contain the word. Review the answer choices to find the most appropriate transition word.

Getting to the Answer: Both sentences are about how the heart supplies the body with blood. The second sentence describes a cause-and-effect relationship between the heart's constant activity and its status as the hardest-working muscle in the body. "Because" is the correct transition word, making (B) the correct answer.

10. C
Difficulty: Medium

Category: Writing & Language / Usage

Strategic Advice: Identify the underlined pronoun's antecedent. If the antecedent is unclear, use a noun instead.

Getting to the Answer: The pronoun does not have a clear antecedent. Context demonstrates that the pronoun refers to the body, because the heart requires "4 to 5 percent" of the blood that is in the body. Choice (C) is correct.

11. A
Difficulty: Medium

Category: Writing & Language / Development

Strategic Advice: Determine what the passage is primarily about, and then summarize the central idea in your own words. Review the answer choices to find the one that best matches your prediction. Avoid selecting answer choices that describe a supporting detail, but not the central idea.

Getting to the Answer: The passage is primarily about how the heart pumps blood through an extensive network of blood vessels, including the heart itself. Choice (A) is correct.

WRITING & LANGUAGE PRACTICE SET 3

Questions 1-11 are based on the following passage.

Motor City, Motown, and Hitsville U.S.A.

From the outside, 2648 West Grand Boulevard in the city of Detroit may not look like much, but the inside was the center of the famed Hitsville U.S.A. offices of Motown Records, one of the most influential and dynamic recording companies in America. Not only were the Motown offices a 24-hour business producing hit records and discovering new talent, but the company also helped develop the careers of budding songwriters, producers, and record executives.

The arrival of the "Motown sound" **1** heralded a new direction in American music and marked the beginnings of "crossover" music, or songs that appeal to many different groups and tastes. Guided by the founder of Motown Records, Berry Gordy, the sound helped fully push African American singers, musicians, and songwriters into the mainstream arena of pop music.

1. A)   NO CHANGE
   B)   borrowed
   C)   canceled
   D)   managed

[1] What made the Motown sound? [2] The songs had memorable lyrics accentuated by hand clapping, tambourines, loud horns, strong bass lines, and drums. [3] Motown music was also distinct for its ongoing back-and-forth interplay between the lead singer and backup vocalists. [4] The music also drew from different influences, including jazz and gospel. [5] All of these elements helped create chart-topping songs recorded by the Supremes, the Four Tops, the Temptations, Stevie Wonder, and the Jackson 5. [6] It is hard to believe that the company was founded with just an $800 family loan. [7] As one magazine writer later stated, "Even if you couldn't put your finger on it, when a Motown song came on, you knew it." **2**

Another important facet of the Motown sound was the studio engineers' ability to understand the audio equipment **3** available, during the onset of Motown, people enjoyed music on stereos and record players, but they also used car radios. Special studio equipment was employed to help Motown engineers figure out how **4** they're music might sound on various **5** lines.

Motown Records was the first African American-owned recording company to reach a wider national audience. It also broke down **6** racial prejudice. With the crossover appeal of its music. Motown Records **7** is becoming the most successful independent record label company in history, as well as

2. Which sentence provides the least support for the central idea of this paragraph?

   A) Sentence 2
   B) Sentence 3
   C) Sentence 5
   D) Sentence 6

3. A) NO CHANGE
   B) available during the onset of Motown
   C) available. During the onset of Motown
   D) available unless during the onset of Motown

4. A) NO CHANGE
   B) its
   C) their
   D) there

5. A) NO CHANGE
   B) accounts
   C) devices
   D) wires

6. A) NO CHANGE
   B) racial prejudice, with the crossover appeal of its music.
   C) racial prejudice; with the crossover appeal of its music.
   D) racial prejudice with the crossover appeal of its music.

7. A) NO CHANGE
   B) became
   C) becomes
   D) had become

the most successful African American-owned business in the country. Motown music later paved the way for other musical styles, including hip hop and rap, as well as the creation of more independent ⑧ record label and recording companies.

⑨ ⑩

8. A) NO CHANGE
    B) record labels'
    C) record label's
    D) record labels

9. Which choice provides the most effective conclusion for this paragraph?

    A) Gordy sold Motown Records to MCA and Boston Partners in 1988.

    B) Motown recording stars were some of the most popular and sought-after singers of that time.

    C) Given the number of ways in which Motown Records made history, its impact on American culture cannot be overstated.

    D) Motown executives often asked teenagers to listen to new recordings and share their opinions of the music.

10. Which choice, if inserted at the beginning of the paragraph, would make the best topic sentence?

    A) Motown had more than 450 employees in 1966.

    B) Motown Records made dramatic progress.

    C) Berry Gordy started as a songwriter for local Detroit musicians.

    D) In 1967, Berry Gordy purchased what is now known as Motown Mansion.

Anyone who grew up listening to Motown music during the 1960s and 1970s will tell you that Motown was not just about music. As one writer noted, Motown was **11** an institution, a state of mind, a way of life, a style the "Sound of Young America."

11. A) NO CHANGE

B) an institution a state of mind, a way of life, a style, the "Sound of Young America."

C) an institution, a state of mind a way of life a style, the "Sound of Young America."

D) an institution, a state of mind, a way of life, a style, the "Sound of Young America."

ANSWERS & EXPLANATIONS

1. A
2. D
3. C
4. C
5. C
6. D
7. B
8. D
9. C
10. B
11. D

1. A
Difficulty: Medium

Category: Writing & Language / Effective Language Use

Strategic Advice: Pretend the underlined word is a blank in the sentence. Then read each answer choice into that blank to determine which one provides the correct connotation in context.

Getting to the Answer: The sentence's connotation, particularly from the word "arrival," suggests a word that means something like "began." The closest match is "heralded," so (A) is correct.

2. D
Category: Writing & Language / Development

Difficulty: Hard

Strategic Advice: To find the correct answer choice, determine which sentence could be omitted from the paragraph without changing the intended meaning.

Getting to the Answer: Sentence 6 is the least essential sentence in the paragraph because the detail about how the company was founded does not contribute to the central idea about how the Motown sound was defined. Choice (D) is correct.

3. C
Difficulty: Medium

Category: Writing & Language / Sentence Formation

Strategic Advice: Two independent clauses should be two separate sentences or joined with a coordinating conjunction. Be wary of inappropriate conjunctions that incorrectly combine sentences.

Getting to the Answer: Choice (C) correctly divides the two thoughts into two complete sentences by adding a period and capitalizing the first letter of the first word in the second sentence.

4. C
Difficulty: Medium

Category: Writing & Language / Usage

Strategic Advice: When you see a word frequently confused with others underlined, make sure the correct word is being used for the context of the sentence.

Getting to the Answer: "There" can be an adjective, adverb, pronoun, or noun; "their" is a possessive pronoun; and "they're" is a contraction of "they are," which is incorrect in this context. The underlined portion should be the possessive plural pronoun "their." Choice (C) is correct.

5. C

Difficulty: Easy

Category: Writing & Language / Effective Language Use

Strategic Advice: Read each word into the sentence in the place of the underlined portion to determine which fits with the context.

Getting to the Answer: The sentence specifically refers to different kinds of equipment, which means "devices" fits the context. Choice (C) is correct.

6. D

Difficulty: Medium

Category: Writing & Language / Punctuation

Strategic Advice: When punctuation is included in an underlined segment, look closely to see if it is incorrect or unnecessary.

Getting to the Answer: The noun phrase "racial prejudice" should not be separated from the prepositional phrase "with the crossover appeal of its music." The period between the noun phrase and the preposition phrase not only incorrectly separates them, but it also renders the prepositional phrase a fragment. Choice (D) correctly removes this unnecessary punctuation.

7. B

Difficulty: Medium

Category: Writing & Language / Shifts in Construction

Strategic Advice: When a verb or simple phrase is underlined, check if its tense is consistent with that of other verbs used in the sentence or paragraph. A shift in verb tense must be warranted by the context of the passage.

Getting to the Answer: The verb phrase "is becoming" is in the present continuous tense.

The other verbs in the paragraph are in the simple past tense (e.g., "was" and "broke down"), so the underlined verb phrase needs to be in the simple past tense as well. Watch out for D, which is the past perfect form of the verb "to become." Choice (B) is correct.

8. D

Difficulty: Easy

Category: Writing & Language / Usage

Strategic Advice: When two noun phrases are modified by the same adjective, the nouns should be in agreement.

Getting to the Answer: There is no need for a possessive form here, so you can eliminate B and C. Reread the two noun phrases modified by "independent" to determine whether the nouns are in agreement. The first noun ("label") is singular, while the second noun ("companies") is plural. They should both agree. Because you cannot change "companies" to a singular noun, "record label" must be plural. Choice (D) is correct.

9. C

Difficulty: Medium

Category: Writing & Language / Development

Strategic Advice: Look for the answer choices that best summarizes the information presented in the paragraph. Eliminate answer choices that contain irrelevant details.

Getting to the Answer: This paragraph is about Motown Records' success and subsequent impact on American culture. Choice (C) provides this summary and is correct.

10. B

Difficulty: Medium

Category: Writing & Language / Organization

Strategic Advice: A good topic sentence will provide a transition from the previous paragraph and an introduction of what this paragraph will discuss.

Getting to the Answer: The previous paragraph mostly discusses the ways in which Motown engineers recorded music based on the equipment available to the average consumer at that time. This paragraph explores the many successes of Motown Records. Choice (B) is correct because it ties the two paragraphs together and sets up the second paragraph with the general statement about Motown Records' "dramatic progress."

11. D

Difficulty: Medium

Category: Writing & Language / Punctuation

Strategic Advice: Words or phrases in a series or list should be separated by commas, even if the last item is not preceded by "and."

Getting to the Answer: As written, this list is missing a comma between "a style" and "the 'Sound of Young America'." While B and C both insert this omitted comma, they remove other commas that are also needed to separate items in this series. Choice (D) is correct.

WRITING & LANGUAGE PRACTICE SET 4

Questions 1-11 are based on the following passage.

Chaka

At the close of the eighteenth century, Southern Africa was a region of constant warfare. It was during this time that one warrior named Chaka, who lived from 1785 to 1828, **1** led his Zulu tribe on a trail of conquest and expansion. In his destructive wake, Chaka created one of the largest empires in African history and changed the face of African warfare. It is no wonder that friend and foe alike referred to Chaka as the "Black Napoleon." **2**

[1] Chaka's success was largely due to innovations in military organization, training, and tactics. [2] Tribal wars had been clumsy affairs, with mobs of warriors randomly throwing spears at each other. [3] In ancient times, spears had been used in combat by Greek and Roman armies. [4] To increase efficiency, Chaka organized the Zulu army into regiments called *impi*, each identified by distinct markings on their shields. [5] Each *impi* was ruled by a commander **3** who was called an *induna* who reported directly to Chaka. [6] This separation into smaller units allowed for greater organization on the

1. A) NO CHANGE
    B) leads
    C) was leading
    D) has been led

2. Which choice provides the best evidence for the claim made at the beginning of this paragraph?

    A) Most people in Southern African subsisted by farming and raising cattle.
    B) The Zulu tribe lived in peace, except for several small disputes over land and resources.
    C) Tribes and clans continually fought and schemed to consolidate their strongholds and destroy their enemies.
    D) In the early nineteenth century, Europe became the battleground of the Napoleonic Wars, which devastated the countryside.

3. A) NO CHANGE
    B) called
    C) who was known as
    D) who would have been called

④ battlefield, and the ability to direct units to specific areas of need. ⑤

The soldiers making up the *impi* were trained in ⑥ a most unique way. ⑦ They suffered through a brutal training program. They ran barefoot for miles at a stretch to build up toughness. Any sign of weakness or fatigue meant instant

4. A) NO CHANGE
   B) battlefield: and the ability
   C) battlefield; and the ability
   D) battlefield and the ability

5. Which sentence could be removed to improve the paragraph's focus?
   A) Sentence 2
   B) Sentence 3
   C) Sentence 4
   D) Sentence 6

6. A) NO CHANGE
   B) a unique
   C) a more unique
   D) an extremely unique

7. Which choice most effectively combines the sentences at the underlined portion?
   A) They suffered through a brutal training program, they ran barefoot for miles at a stretch to build up toughness.
   B) They suffered through a brutal training program, and ran barefoot for miles at a stretch to build up toughness.
   C) They suffered through a brutal training program, running barefoot for miles at a stretch to build up toughness.
   D) They suffered through a brutal training program, and running barefoot for miles at a stretch to build up toughness.

death, a cruel policy that created a ⑧ resolute corps of warriors. ⑨ Actually, the Zulus were equipped with more advanced
weapons than other tribes. Instead of clumsy throwing spears,
Zulu soldiers carried short stabbing spears and full-length
cowhide shields. ⑩ These were perfectly suited for the hand-
to-hand combat Chaka utilized in their battlefield strategy.

[1] That strategy, known as the impondo zankomo, or
"bull's horns," converted Chaka's concepts into victory on the
battlefield. [2] Fast-moving impi would form two long col-
umns, or "horns," that would rush out and surround the enemy
army on each side. [3] The force of these "horns" would push
the enemy toward the main body of the army, or the "bull's
head." [4] Surrounded and incapable of countering Chaka's
battle tactics, the enemy would be annihilated. [5] The survi-
vors could then choose to either join with Chaka and the Zulus
or die. [6] The Zulu army, which started with only 350 men in
1808, grew to 2,000 warriors by 1820 and to almost 40,000 by
his death in 1828. [7] In all, the Zulus killed almost 2 million
people during Chaka's reign, securing Zulu dominance in
Africa for another half-century. ⑪

8. A) NO CHANGE
   B) mortal
   C) stern
   D) ruthless

9. A) NO CHANGE
   B) In addition
   C) Therefore
   D) On the other hand

10. A) NO CHANGE
    B) It was perfectly suited for
        the hand-to-hand combat
        Chaka utilized in their bat-
        tlefield strategy.
    C) It was perfectly suited for
        the hand-to-hand combat
        Chaka utilized in his bat-
        tlefield strategy.
    D) These were perfectly suited
        for the hand-to-hand com-
        bat Chaka utilized in his
        battlefield strategy.

11. To make this paragraph most
    logical, sentence 3 should be
    placed
    A) where it is now.
    B) after sentence 1.
    C) after sentence 4.
    D) after sentence 5.

ANSWERS & EXPLANATIONS

1. A
2. C
3. B
4. D
5. B
6. B
7. C
8. D
9. B
10. D
11. A

1. A
Difficulty: Easy

Category: Writing & Language / Shifts in Construction

Strategic Advice: Make sure the underlined verb is consistent with the other verbs used throughout the paragraph.

Getting to the Answer: The other verbs in the paragraph are in the simple past tense. "Led" is also in the simple past tense; therefore, the verb tense does not shift and the underlined portion is correct as written. Choice (A) is correct.

2. C
Difficulty: Hard

Category: Writing & Language / Development

Strategic Advice: Identify the central claim of the paragraph, then select the answer choice that provides evidence directly supporting that claim.

Getting to the Answer: The central claim of the paragraph is that "Southern Africa was a region of constant warfare" near the end of the eighteenth century. Only (C) provides specific details regarding the reasons for the warfare, and is therefore correct.

3. B
Difficulty: Easy

Category: Writing & Language / Effective Language Use

Strategic Advice: Read each answer choice into the sentence and select the one that expresses the idea in the clearest, most concise manner. Watch out for answer choices that use unnecessary words.

Getting to the Answer: As written, this sentence is overly wordy. Neither C nor D corrects this error. Choice (B), "called," expresses the idea without using extra words and is therefore correct.

4. D
Difficulty: Medium

Category: Writing & Language / Punctuation

Strategic Advice: Read the entire sentence containing the underlined portion. Determine whether there are multiple elements in the sentence that should be separated by punctuation.

Getting to the Answer: The sentence contains a preposition ("for") with a compound object. The phrase "greater organization on the battlefield" is the first of two elements in the compound; the second is "the ability to direct units to specific areas of need." Because there are only two elements, punctuation is not needed to separate them. Choice (D) is correct.

5. B

Difficulty: Hard

Category: Writing & Language / Development

Strategic Advice: Determine the central idea of the paragraph, then check each answer choice to make sure it supports that idea. The answer choice that is least related to the central idea will be correct.

Getting to the Answer: The central idea of this paragraph is expressed in the topic sentence: Chaka's success was based on his military innovations. Sentences 2, 4, and 6 provide support for this idea, but Sentence 3, which discusses spear use in ancient Greece and Rome, is off-topic. Choice (B) is correct.

6. B

Difficulty: Medium

Category: Writing & Language / Usage

Strategic Advice: Determine whether the words in the underlined phrase make sense together; if not, select the answer choice that provides a more logical substitution.

Getting to the Answer: To call something "unique" means that it is the only one of its kind. It does not make sense to say that one type of training is "most unique" or "more unique." Choice (B) is correct.

7. C

Difficulty: Hard

Category: Writing & Language / Sentence Formation

Strategic Advice: Reread the sentences to determine how to best logically combine them. The correct answer will make the relationship between the two sentences clear.

Getting to the Answer: The best way to combine the sentences is by turning one of them into a modifying phrase. Choice (C) is correct because "running barefoot for miles at a stretch to build up toughness" describes how the soldiers were trained.

8. D

Difficulty: Hard

Category: Writing & Language / Effective Language Use

Strategic Advice: Read the entire sentence, looking for context clues. Predict a word that would fit into the underlined portion, and then scan the answer choices to find the one that most closely matches your prediction.

Getting to the Answer: You can predict that a "cruel" policy would create warriors who were "savage," or "ruthless." Choice (D) is correct. Watch out for answer choices like C, "stern," that are plausible but not the most precise choice.

9. B

Difficulty: Medium

Category: Writing & Language / Organization

Strategic Advice: Look for the relationship between this sentence and the previous one. Next, review the answer choices to find a transition word or phrase that shows this relationship. Read the word or phrase into the sentence to make sure that it conveys the author's intended meaning.

Getting to the Answer: The sentence provides information that builds upon the information in the previous sentence. The transition phrase "In addition" shows this relationship. Choice (B) is correct.

10. D

Difficulty: Hard

Category: Writing & Language / Usage

Strategic Advice: Notice the pronouns in the underlined sentence. Determine that each pronoun matches its antecedent in person and number.

Getting to the Answer: The pronouns in the underlined sentence are "these" and "their." The antecedent for "these" is "short stabbing spears and full-length cowhide shields." Both the antecedent and the pronoun are plural and third-person, so "these" is correct. The antecedent for "their" is "Chaka," which is singular third-person and should be followed by the singular third-person pronoun "his." Therefore, (D) is correct.

11. A

Difficulty: Medium

Category: Writing & Language / Organization

Strategic Advice: Notice that sentences 2 through 5 describe steps in a process. Make sure that the step described in sentence 3 logically follows the one before it.

Getting to the Answer: The paragraph describes how the "bull's horns" strategy worked. First the *impi* would form two long "horns" that would surround the enemy (sentence 2). Then the "horns" would push the enemy toward the main fighting force (sentence 3). Once the enemy was surrounded, they would be killed or forced to join Chaka's army (sentences 4 and 5). The paragraph expresses these steps in the most logical order; therefore, (A) is correct.

WRITING & LANGUAGE PRACTICE SET 5

Questions 1-11 are based on the following passage.

Eye on the World: The Professional Photographer

Whether it is ❶ a wedding, a newborn baby, the weekly football game; or life in a war zone, ❷ there is no shortage of opportunities for a photographer to pursue a passion for taking pictures. Photographers play an important role, for they create permanent images for a wide range of occasions. If anything, new directions in photography are being created more than ever before, allowing for fresh ways of exploring the world behind the lens of a camera.

Most professional photographers develop a specialty, ❸ in such categories as photographing weddings, children, pets, or families. Others focus on advertising, taking pictures of food or the latest fashions. Then there are photographers who ❹ had worked for magazines and newspapers that document world events and people. Fine art photographers will often be

1. A) NO CHANGE
   B) a wedding, a newborn baby, the weekly football game, or life in a war zone,
   C) a wedding; a newborn baby; the weekly football game; or life in a war zone
   D) a wedding, a newborn baby, the weekly football game; or life in a war zone

2. A) NO CHANGE
   B) there are
   C) there was
   D) there were

3. A) NO CHANGE
   B) as
   C) such as
   D) such as these categories, for example:

4. A) NO CHANGE
   B) work
   C) worked
   D) were working

found experimenting with new techniques and materials to create exciting and innovative works of art. [5]

For Evan Harrison, who works as a wildlife [6] photographer. There was never any doubt about what she would do for a living.

"I am passionate about animals and the environment," says Harrison. "Being able to document animals and their world is not only about educating people, but also about showing that animals need to have their world intact to survive, too."

5. Which sentence, if added, would best support the central idea of this paragraph?

A) Stock-photo clearinghouses compile a wide range of pictures of a variety of subjects.

B) Digital photography allows many hobby photographers to make money through sales of their pictures.

C) Portrait photography is typically more lucrative than fine art photography and is less grueling than photojournalism.

D) Some photographers specialize in nature photography, capturing images of wildlife and flora for scientific documentation.

6. A) NO CHANGE
   B) photographer there
   C) photographer, there
   D) photographer; there

Harrison studied photography in school, earning a Bachelor of Fine Arts degree with an emphasis on photography. But, she cautions, photographers need to know more than just how to take a picture; Harrison also took courses to learn how to use software for editing and storing her photographs. [7]

"Knowing how to use the software to 'develop' your pictures is [8] optional," she says. "You could have the million-dollar shot; but if you do not know how to edit it properly, it will make no difference as to how great it is, if it does not look good."

Harrison also stresses that although school can provide the [9] foundation, becoming a professional photographer is also about learning on the job.

7. Which of the following most effectively conveys the central idea of this paragraph?
   A) Photographers cannot simply rely on their skill behind the lens to be successful.
   B) Many photographers had careers in other fields before they studied photography.
   C) Photographers face an increasingly unstable job market due to the number of hobbyists taking their own pictures.
   D) A flood of images available inexpensively via stock-photo subscriptions has reduced the profitability of commercial photography.

8. A) NO CHANGE
   B) crucial
   C) forgivable
   D) variable

9. A) NO CHANGE
   B) origin
   C) formation
   D) infrastructure

"My first job was with a nature conservancy group that wanted to document the wildlife living in a marsh area. I had to quickly figure out not only the equipment and proper clothing I needed, but also gain an understanding of the environment I was about to work in."

Some of Harrison's jobs take her to different parts of the world, which means she must educate herself about the people and the culture to facilitate communication. "Communicating with people is critical; it can often mean the difference between getting a good shot and a great shot of an area," she notes. **10**

Knowing how to be quiet is essential, too. "Animals have keen **11** hearing: so it does not pay to make a lot of noise if you hope to capture wildlife," Harrison adds, laughing.

10. Which sentence, if inserted at this point, would provide the most support for the central idea of the paragraph?

A) People can be resistant to an outsider documenting their homeland and the wildlife there.

B) Often it can be difficult to obtain appropriate lodging in remote locations without personal connections to people who live there.

C) Harrison frequently contacts government authorities to obtain proper permits and clearances prior to photographing animals in the wild.

D) For example, Harrison won awards for a photograph of the birth of a rare rhino, an event she witnessed due to a tip from a local contact in Namibia.

11. A) NO CHANGE
    B) hearing, so
    C) hearing; so
    D) hearing so

ANSWERS & EXPLANATIONS

1. B
2. A
3. C
4. B
5. D
6. C
7. A
8. B
9. A
10. D
11. B

1. B
Difficulty: Hard

Category: Writing & Language / Punctuation

Strategic Advice: Identify each of the items in the list, and analyze the series to determine proper punctuation. Consider the relationship between the clause containing the series and the clause that follows it.

Getting to the Answer: The SAT requires commas after each item in a list of three or more items. In this case, the final item in the list requires a comma because the series is part of a conditional dependent clause starting with "whether." Choice (B) is correct.

2. A
Difficulty: Medium

Category: Writing & Language / Usage

Strategic Advice: Reread the sentence to identify the antecedent of the pronoun "there" and the verb tense for the initial clause. Make sure the pronoun matches the antecedent in number and that tense is the same throughout the sentence.

Getting to the Answer: The singular verb "is" should be used for the pronoun "there." "There" is singular because it is referring to "a shortage." The tense should be present to match "whether it is" in the initial clause, so the underlined portion is correct as written. Choice (A) is correct.

3. C
Difficulty: Medium

Category: Writing & Language / Effective Language Use

Strategic Advice: Think about whether the underlined words express the idea in the most concise way possible. Then review the answer choices to see if another choice is more concise.

Getting to the Answer: When wordiness or redundancy is being tested, do not automatically select the shortest answer choice. While B, "as," is the most concise answer choice, it is incorrect because it turns the sentence into a fragment. The phrase "such as" introduces the list of specialties in the most concise way while conveying the intended meaning and maintaining grammatical correctness. Choice (C) is correct.

4. B
Difficulty: Easy

Category: Writing & Language / Shifts in Construction

Strategic Advice: Review the paragraph to assess which verb tenses are used. The verb tense should not change unless warranted by the context.

Getting to the Answer: The underlined verb phrase, "had worked," is in the past perfect tense but the other verbs in the paragraph are in the present tense, so the underlined phrase should be "work." Choice (B) is correct.

5. D
Difficulty: Hard

Category: Writing & Language / Development

Strategic Advice: Identify the paragraph's central idea, then determine which answer choice would best support it.

Getting to the Answer: The central idea of the paragraph is about how most photographers develop a specialty. Choice (D) supports that idea by offering a specific example of a type of photography specialization, and is therefore correct.

6. C
Difficulty: Medium

Category: Writing & Language / Sentence Formation

Strategic Advice: A complete sentence needs to use a subject and a predicate verb to express a complete thought.

Getting to the Answer: As written, the first sentence in the paragraph is a sentence fragment because it does not have a predicate verb. Deleting the period and adding a comma between the first and second sentences creates a correctly formed single sentence that contains one complete thought. Choice (C) is correct.

7. A
Difficulty: Medium

Category: Writing & Language / Development

Strategic Advice: Analyze the body sentences of the paragraph. The supporting details found in the body sentences of a paragraph will help you determine the central idea.

Getting to the Answer: The sentence that conveys the central idea must establish that a range of skills is required to be a photographer. Choice (A) is correct.

8. B
Difficulty: Medium

Category: Writing & Language / Effective Language Use

Strategic Advice: Review the paragraph for context clues and predict a word that would make sense in place of the underlined word. Evaluate each answer choice and select the one that best matches your prediction.

Getting to the Answer: The paragraph describes how photographers need to have editing skills to create great photographs. The underlined word should convey something like "really important" because Harrison states photographs cannot look good without decent editing. Choice (B) is correct because it matches this prediction.

9. A
Difficulty: Hard

Category: Writing & Language / Effective Language Use

Strategic Advice: Summarize the idea being conveyed in the sentences before and after the sentence containing the underlined word. Use this summary to determine which answer choice conveys the intended meaning.

Getting to the Answer: Harrison says school is important, but she also states that a formal education is not the only criterion needed to be a good photographer. The underlined word, "foundation," conveys this meaning so it is correct as written. Choice (A) is correct.

10. D

Difficulty: Medium

Category: Writing & Language / Development

Strategic Advice: First, identify the central idea of the paragraph. Then, look for a sentence among the answer choices that offers details supporting that idea.

Getting to the Answer: The first sentence in this paragraph states that communication is an important part of a photographer's job. Choice (D) is correct because it gives a specific example of how communication resulted in a prize-winning photograph.

11. B

Difficulty: Easy

Category: Writing & Language / Punctuation

Strategic Advice: When you see a conjunction in an underlined segment, determine whether the phrase that follows it is an independent clause.

Getting to the Answer: The underlined segment contains a colon that is used incorrectly to combine the two independent clauses. A comma is need to correctly separate two independent clauses linked by the coordinating conjunction "so." Choice (B) is correct.

WRITING & LANGUAGE PRACTICE SET 6

Questions 1-11 are based on the following passage and supplementary material.

The History of Smallpox

For thousands of years, smallpox was one of the world's most dreaded diseases. **1** A solidly infectious disease spread by a virus, smallpox was the scourge of medieval Europe, where it was known by **2** their symptoms of extreme fever and disfiguring rash as "the invisible fire." In many outbreaks, mortality rates were higher than 25 percent. Ancient Chinese medical texts show that the disease was known as long ago as 1122 BCE. But as recently as 1967, more than 2 million people died of smallpox in one year.

The first method developed to combat smallpox was an attempt to immunize healthy patients. In a procedure called *variolation*, known since the ninth century CE, a healthy patient's skin was deliberately scratched with infectious material from a person with a mild case of smallpox. **3** Before the treatment was successful, the patient suffered a mild smallpox infection and then **4** became immune to the disease. By the eighteenth century, when smallpox epidemics were regular occurrences, *variolation* was a common practice among the wealthy and aristocratic. Unfortunately, *variolation* sometimes led to severe, even fatal, infections. Moreover, even if it was successful, the patient could spread smallpox to others.

A safer method of conferring immunity was discovered in 1796 by an English doctor named Edward Jenner. Jenner, who had himself undergone the *variolation* process as a child, was fascinated by the fact that people who caught cowpox, a

1. A) NO CHANGE
   B) An acutely
   C) A mildly
   D) An ominously

2. A) NO CHANGE
   B) they're
   C) its
   D) it's

3. A) NO CHANGE
   B) Whether the treatment was successful,
   C) And the treatment was successful,
   D) If the treatment was successful,

4. A) NO CHANGE
   B) becomes
   C) had become
   D) was becoming

harmless disease spread by cattle, became immune to smallpox. To test whether this immunity could be replicated, Jenner inoculated a young boy with infectious matter ⑤ taken from a child, who had cowpox. The boy developed a slight infection. Later, Jenner inoculated the boy with smallpox matter and discovered that no disease developed. Jenner wrote a paper describing his results, but the Royal Society of Physicians, who were ⑥ offended by his unconventional approach, rejected it. Jenner published his findings independently, and his paper became a bestseller. Within a matter of years, the new procedure, known as vaccination, was in general use throughout Europe and the United States, and the fight against smallpox was underway.

[1] It was not until 1966, ⑦ however, that the World Health Organization was able to find the resources to launch a worldwide campaign to wipe out the disease altogether. [2] ⑧ It was an immense project involving thousands of health workers. WHO teams moved from country to country, locating every case of active smallpox and vaccinating all potential contacts. [3] In 1977, the last active case of smallpox was

5. A) NO CHANGE
   B) taken from a child who had cowpox.
   C) taken from a child: who had cowpox.
   D) taken from a child; who had cowpox.

6. A) NO CHANGE
   B) enthusiastic about
   C) skeptical about
   D) intrigued by

7. A) NO CHANGE
   B) naturally
   C) specifically
   D) similarly

8. Which choice most effectively combines the sentences in the underlined portion?
   A) Although it was an immense project involving thousands of health workers, WHO teams moved from country to country,
   B) It was an immense project involving thousands of health workers, whenever WHO teams moved from country to country,
   C) Instead of an immense project involving thousands of health workers, WHO teams moved from country to country,
   D) In an immense project involving thousands of health workers, WHO teams moved from country to country,

found and eliminated. [4] Because there are no animal carriers of smallpox, the WHO was able to declare in 1980 that the dreaded killer had been conquered. [5] For the first time in the history of medicine, a disease had been completely eradiated from the human population. **9 10 11**

Number Smallpox Cases and Fatalities Worldwide, 1950–1975		
Years	# of Cases	# of Fatalities
1950–1954	72,181	48,815
1955–1959	125,916	90,697
1960–1964	6,979	5,008
1965–1969	21,135	9,709
1970–1975	84,930	18,390

9. Which sentence best expresses the central idea of the paragraph?

    A) Sentence 1

    B) Sentence 2

    C) Sentence 3

    D) Sentence 5

10. According to the table, prior to the start of the worldwide campaign to eliminate smallpox, when was the number of smallpox fatalities highest relative to the number of cases reported?

    A) 1950–1954

    B) 1955–1959

    C) 1960–1964

    D) 1970–1975

11. Based on the information in the table and the passage, during the two decades prior to the eradication of smallpox, the number of cases

    A) steadily increased.

    B) steadily decreased.

    C) increased and then decreased.

    D) decreased and then increased.

ANSWERS & EXPLANATIONS

1. B
2. C
3. D
4. A
5. B
6. C
7. A
8. D
9. D
10. C
11. D

1. B
Difficulty: Hard

Category: Writing & Language / Effective Language Use

Strategic Advice: Look for context clues to understand how the underlined phrase is used in the sentence. Then, evaluate the answer choices to determine which is correct.

Getting to the Answer: The underlined phrase, "A solidly," describes the progression of a disease that disfigured people and caused high mortality rates. The word "acutely" fits this context because "acute" means "sharp" or "severe." Therefore, (B) is correct.

2. C
Difficulty: Medium

Category: Writing & Language / Usage

Strategic Advice: When the underlined word is a pronoun, find its antecedent to make sure the pronoun matches it in person and number. If it does not match, search for the correct pronoun among the answer choices.

Getting to the Answer: "Their" is incorrect because the antecedent is "smallpox." The correct pronoun should be singular, making (C), "its," the correct answer choice.

3. D
Difficulty: Medium

Category: Writing & Language / Sentence Formation

Strategic Advice: Reread the underlined portion of the sentence to determine whether it is an independent or dependent clause. Dependent clauses must be preceded by a subordinating conjunction.

Getting to the Answer: The sentence explains that the result of a successful treatment was that the patient suffered a slight infection and then developed immunity to the disease. The subordinating conjunction needs to show that the second part of the sentence is dependent on the first. "If" shows the correct relationship; therefore, (D) is correct.

4. A
Difficulty: Easy

Category: Writing & Language / Usage

Strategic Advice: Pay attention to the verb tenses in the sentence to which the underlined portion belongs. Verbs within a sentence should be in the same tense unless a tense shift is required by the context.

Getting to the Answer: The other verbs in the sentence ("was" and "suffered") are in the simple past tense. The underlined verb, "became," is also be in the simple past tense, so no change is necessary. Choice (A) is correct.

5. B

Difficulty: Medium

Category: Writing & Language / Punctuation

Strategic Advice: When the underlined portion of the sentence contains a dependent clause, read the entire sentence to determine whether the dependent clause contains essential or nonessential information. If the information is nonessential, punctuation should be used to set off the clause.

Getting to the Answer: The dependent clause "who had cowpox" is essential to the meaning of the sentence. Without that information, it would seem as if the infectious matter could be taken from any child. Because the information is essential, punctuation should not be used in the underlined portion. Choice (B) is correct.

6. C

Difficulty: Hard

Category: Writing & Language / Effective Language Use

Strategic Advice: Read the sentence for context clues to understand the intended meaning of the underlined word.

Getting to the Answer: The sentence describes how the Royal Society of Physicians "rejected" Jenner's paper. This context clue indicates that the underlined words will have a somewhat negative charge. While A, "offended by," may seem plausible at first, it is too extreme for the context of the sentence. Choice (C), "skeptical about," is a better fit in the context of a decision made by physicians and is therefore correct.

7. A

Difficulty: Medium

Category: Writing & Language / Organization

Strategic Advice: Read the last sentence in the paragraph before the underlined word to determine the type of transition needed.

Getting to the Answer: The transition word needs to indicate a contrast: while vaccinations for smallpox began around 1800, it took more than 150 years before a serious campaign was launched to eliminate the disease. This contrast is best shown by the transition word "however," so the underlined portion is correct as written. Choice (A) is correct.

8. D

Difficulty: Hard

Category: Writing & Language / Sentence Formation

Strategic Advice: Read the two sentences and determine the relationship between them. Two sentences that are closely related may be combined by turning one of them into a phrase or dependent clause. Watch out for answer choices that alter the intended meaning.

Getting to the Answer: The second sentence builds upon the first by providing more information about the project. Choice (D) is correct because it turns the first sentence into an introductory phrase that flows into the next sentence while retaining the intended meaning.

9. D

Difficulty: Medium

Category: Writing & Language / Development

Strategic Advice: Summarize the paragraph in your own words and select the answer choice that best expresses this idea. Be sure your choice reflects the central idea, and not a supporting detail.

Getting to the Answer: The central idea of the paragraph is that smallpox was completely eradicated. Sentences 1, 2, and 3 provide details that explain how this was achieved. Only sentence 5 expresses the central idea. Choice (D) is correct.

10. C
Difficulty: Hard

Category: Writing & Language / Quantitative

Strategic Advice: Pay attention to key words and phrases in the question stem that can help you eliminate incorrect answer choices.

Getting to the Answer: To answer this question correctly, you must first identify the year the worldwide campaign to eliminate smallpox began. Review the passage to find this information, and then study each answer choice in the infographic before answering this question. According to the passage, the worldwide campaign to eliminate smallpox began in 1966. This allows you to eliminate D, 1970–1975, which is after 1966. The table shows that 1960–1964 had the highest number of deaths relative to the number of cases. Choice (C) is correct.

11. D
Difficulty: Medium

Category: Writing & Language / Quantitative

Strategic Advice: Quantitative questions often require you to synthesize information from the passage and the presented data.

Getting to the Answer: To answer this question correctly, you will need to find the part of the passage that discusses the year the smallpox was eliminated. Then find the data in the table that pertain to the twenty years before the eradication of smallpox. The passage states that smallpox was eradicated in 1977. The last four rows of the table contain data about the twenty years prior to this date. Cases of smallpox decreased dramatically, then increased, making (D) the correct answer.

WRITING & LANGUAGE PRACTICE SET 7

Questions 1-11 are based on the following passage.

The Evolution of Dance: Classical to Modern

Modern dance and classical ballet are two very different forms of dance, residing on opposite ends of the formal **❶** realm. Despite their differences, because modern dance was born as a reaction to classical ballet, in a sense they have a common origin.

In the sixteenth century, Catherine de Medici, an Italian noblewoman and a great patron of the arts, began funding ballet in the French court. The programs of dance, costume, song, music, and poetry that were put on at her festivals came to be called *ballet de cour*. A century later, King Louis XIV of France popularized the form by dancing **❷** himself, and his love of ballet elevated it from pastime for amateurs to an endeavor requiring professional training. **3**

1. A) NO CHANGE
   B) spectrum
   C) width
   D) extent

2. A) NO CHANGE
   B) himself so
   C) himself, although
   D) himself; however,

3. Which choice, if inserted at the beginning of this paragraph, would be the most effective topic sentence?

   A) Modern dance has many elements in common with ballet, which was first popularized during the Italian Renaissance in the fifteenth century.

   B) Ballet began during the Renaissance and proved very popular in the courts and with the common citizens of fifteenth-century Italy.

   C) Ballet originated in the Italian Renaissance courts of the fifteenth century, when noblemen and women incorporated dance and music into celebrations.

   D) Many contemporary modern dance forms can be traced back to the forms of the ballet that first appeared in Italy during the fifteenth century.

In the nineteenth century, during ballet's Romantic movement, dancing on the tips of the toes, known as *pointe*, became the norm in ballet. The popularity of ballet soared in Russia, where choreographers and composers took it to new heights in works such as *The Nutcracker* and *Swan Lake*, which represent classical ballet in **4** her grandest form, displaying pointe work and precision of movement.

Modern dance began in Europe in the early 1900s and flourished in areas of the United States that did not have a strong ballet tradition. A theatrical form of dance, it is enormously varied, but is primarily defined by its different choreography. **5** Whereas classical ballet works from a catalog of codified steps, modern dance created its own language. **6** For example, because a ballet dancer creates an impression

4. A) NO CHANGE
   B) their
   C) his
   D) its

5. A) NO CHANGE
   B) Whereas classical ballet worked from a catalog of codified steps, modern dance is creating its own language.
   C) Whereas classical ballet works from a catalog of codified steps, modern dance creates its own language.
   D) Whereas classical ballet worked from a catalog of codified steps, modern dance creates its own language.

6. A) NO CHANGE
   B) For example, considering a ballet dancer
   C) For example, many a ballet dancer
   D) For example, while a ballet dancer

of constant lightness, the weight of a modern dancer's body is generally expressed. [7]

The members of a production in modern dance function differently. Unlike ballet [8] <u>choreographers, who do not</u>

7. Which choice, if added at this point, provides the most support for the central idea of this paragraph?

A) The choreography of ballet is generally very different from the choreography associated with modern dance.

B) Ballet's movements are usually sinuous and graceful; modern dance may be anything at all, as long as it is expressive.

C) The language of modern dance has a strong basis—the established tradition of ballet dating from Renaissance Europe.

D) The forms of modern dance continue to evolve today, although emphasis on the weight of the body remains common.

8. A) NO CHANGE

B) choreographers who do not perform in the production, a modern

C) choreographers; who do not perform in the production, a modern

D) choreographers, who do not perform in the production; a modern perform in the production, a modern choreographer ⑨ will often choreograph and performs.

In traditional ballet, dance movements are typically parallel to the rhythms of the music, but in modern dance, the dance may be composed first and the music written afterward, underscoring the impulses of the dance movement, or the momentum of the dance may run counter to the rhythms of the music. Music may even be absent with the sounds of the dancers' movements being heard against a backdrop of silence.

Though classical and contemporary dance are extreme ⑩ opposites; they are forever linked through their shared origin. ⑪

9. A) NO CHANGE
    B) often choreographs and perform
    C) will often choreograph and perform
    D) will often choreographs and performs

10. A) NO CHANGE
    B) opposites, they
    C) opposites. They
    D) opposites: they

11. Which choice most effectively concludes the paragraph and the passage?
    A) Classical dance forms as such as ballet have significantly impacted the development of contemporary dance in the United States.
    B) Many Americans have practiced some form of modern dance at least once thanks to the influence of ballet.
    C) Ballet and contemporary dance are both dance forms that use the body to express feelings.
    D) The precision of ballet and the energy of modern dance were both born from the expressive energy and beauty of the human body.

ANSWERS & EXPLANATIONS

1. B
2. A
3. C
4. D
5. C
6. D
7. B
8. A
9. C
10. B
11. D

1. B
Difficulty: Medium

Category: Writing & Language / Effective Language Use

Strategic Advice: Determine how the word is used in the sentence by rereading the sentence for context clues. Substitute each answer choice to see which works best in context.

Getting to the Answer: The phrase "opposite ends" in the sentence implies that modern dance and classical ballet are compared on a range of different forms of dance. Choice (B) is correct because it compares the two forms of dance relative to others.

2. A
Difficulty: Hard

Category: Writing & Language / Sentence Formation

Strategic Advice: Notice that the two parts of the sentence joined by the comma are clauses. Identify whether each clause is independent or dependent, and then select the answer choice that creates the most logical and grammatically correct sentence.

Getting to the Answer: Although the context of the second clause naturally follows the first, both clauses are independent. A comma must separate two independent clauses of equal importance if they are joined by a coordinating conjunction. Choice (A) is correct because it sets off the first clause with a comma and follows with the coordinating conjunction "and."

3. C
Difficulty: Hard

Category: Writing & Language / Development

Strategic Advice: Summarize the focus of the paragraph based on the details. Determine which answer choice is the best introduction to the information in the paragraph.

Getting to the Answer: The paragraph illustrates how Catherine de Medici and Louis XIV, two members of the nobility, popularized ballet. Eliminate answer choices that include elements that are not present in the body of the paragraph. Choice (C) is correct because it establishes the link between nobility and the development of early ballet, which is the focus of the rest of the paragraph.

4. D
Difficulty: Easy

Category: Writing & Language / Usage

Strategic Advice: Find the antecedent of the underlined possessive pronoun to make sure it agrees in person and number.

Getting to the Answer: The antecedent to "her" is "classical ballet." The noun is singular and does not refer to a person, therefore the correct possessive pronoun is "its." Choice (D) is correct.

5. C

Difficulty: Hard

Category: Writing & Language / Shifts in Construction

Strategic Advice: Review the paragraph's context to determine the correct verb tenses for the underlined sentence. Avoid answer choices in which the verb tense is not consistent.

Getting to the Answer: The preceding sentence is in the present tense, and the underlined sentence also describes the present; therefore, the verbs in this sentence should all be in the present tense. Choice (C) is correct because both verbs are in the present tense.

6. D

Difficulty: Medium

Category: Writing & Language / Effective Language Use

Strategic Advice: Substitute each answer choice to see which works best in the context of the sentence.

Getting to the Answer: The sentence is contrasting ballet dancers and modern dancers. The word "while" in (D) contrasts a modern dancer's emphasis on the weight of the body with a ballet dancer's desire to appear weightless. The other answer choices do not establish a contrast. Choice (D) is correct.

7. B

Difficulty: Hard

Category: Writing & Language / Development

Strategic Advice: Identify the central idea of the paragraph and the details that provide support for that idea. Think about how the elements in each answer choice connect to the rest of the paragraph.

Getting to the Answer: The paragraph is mostly about how the choreography of modern dance is different from the choreography of ballet. Avoid choices like A that summarize the central idea but do not provide supporting details. Choice (B) is correct because it provides details that support this idea.

8. A

Difficulty: Medium

Category: Writing & Language / Punctuation

Strategic Advice: Carefully review the sentence as written to determine if there is an error in punctuation. Identify whether there is a dependent clause that is not essential to the meaning of the sentence.

Getting to the Answer: The additional description of ballet choreographers is a nonessential clause because it is not necessary in the sentence. The use of two commas appropriately sets apart this description from the rest of this sentence, so it is correct as written. Choice (A) is correct.

9. C

Difficulty: Medium

Category: Writing & Language / Usage

Strategic Advice: Identify the subject of the independent clause. Then, predict the verb forms that would agree with the subject in number.

Getting to the Answer: The subject in the independent clause, "choreographer," is singular and paired with two verbs, "choreograph" and "perform." Choice (C) is correct because the number of the noun agrees with both verb forms.

10. B

Difficulty: Easy

Category: Writing & Language / Punctuation

Strategic Advice: Review the sentence for any mistakes in punctuation. Identify how the dependent clause functions in the sentence.

Getting to the Answer: The comma in (B) correctly sets off the dependent clause from the independent clause in the sentence. Choice (B) is correct.

11. D

Difficulty: Hard

Category: Expression of Ideas / Development

Strategic Advice: Read the answer choices into the context of the paragraph and the passage as a whole. An effective concluding sentence will clearly convey information expressed in both.

Getting to the Answer: An effective concluding sentence will reference both classical and modern dance and descriptively allude to the way in which both dance forms are connected in the concluding paragraph and throughout the passage. Choice (D) is correct.

WRITING & LANGUAGE PRACTICE SET 8

Questions 1-11 are based on the following passage.

Paul Revere

Paul Revere has long been venerated as a folk hero of the American Revolution almost solely for his dramatic midnight ride through Boston-area towns, to warn residents that British forces were moving into the city. This famous journey was **❶ immortalized** in a ballad by poet Henry Wadsworth Longfellow. Yet many historians have since suggested that it was this poem itself that created Revere's fame, not his midnight ride. These historians diminish the importance of his role **❷ that night. Citing the fact** that Revere was the only one of the three men sent out on that mission to be captured by the British. However, despite the existence of historical evidence supporting such criticism of his legacy, the more one digs into Revere's contributions to the American Revolution, the clearer **❸ one's** patriotism and dedication to the independence movement become.

[1] Revere did indeed issue important warnings that night, alerting his countrymen that the "redcoats" were on the march, but he was not alone in this effort. [2] Revere rode through the towns along with William Dawes and Samuel Prescott shouting, "The British are coming." [3] They borrowed fresh horses along the way to keep up their speed. [4] Shortly after midnight, the three were **❹ interrupted** by the British just outside of Concord, and, while Dawes and Prescott escaped and rode on, Revere was taken into custody and relieved of his horse. [5]

1. A) NO CHANGE
   B) studied
   C) enacted
   D) encapsulated

2. A) NO CHANGE
   B) that night citing the fact
   C) that night, citing the fact
   D) that night; citing the fact

3. A) NO CHANGE
   B) its
   C) his
   D) their

4. A) NO CHANGE
   B) apprehended
   C) approached
   D) identified

While he certainly failed to complete his prescribed mission, Revere's efforts that night cannot be entirely diminished. [6] Because of his warnings, the Lexington Minutemen were ready the next morning on the town green to face off against the British and launch the War of Independence. [7] He was eventually released but was forced to return to Lexington on foot. **5**

Revere's involvement in the revolution, however, was not limited to the night of April 18, 1775, to which Revere owes his fame. **6** Therefore, when all of Revere's contributions to the American Revolution are considered, that night actually takes a back seat. **7** Revere made his patriotism apparent, while distinguishing himself as a leading silversmith of the colonial era, in his intricately engraved copper plates, the most famous

5. To make this paragraph most logical, sentence 7 should be placed

A) where it is now.

B) after sentence 2.

C) after sentence 4.

D) after sentence 5.

6. A) NO CHANGE

B) However

C) Nevertheless

D) In fact

7. A) NO CHANGE

B) Revere made his patriotism apparent in his intricately engraved copper plates, while distinguishing himself as a leading silversmith of the colonial era,

C) While distinguishing himself as a leading silversmith of the colonial era, Revere made his patriotism apparent in his intricately engraved copper plates,

D) In his intricately engraved copper plates, Revere made his patriotism apparent, while distinguishing himself as a leading silversmith of the colonial era,

of which depicts his version of the **8** Boston Massacre, when British troops fired upon a group of civilian protesters. In the 1770s, as tensions between the colonies and the British crown **9** have increased, Revere totally immersed himself in the movement towards political independence from Great Britain. He enthusiastically participated in numerous demonstrations against the British. His prolific service in the revolution reached its apex when he was given command of the principal defensive fort protecting Boston Harbor. **10** Revere's service to

8. A) NO CHANGE

   B) Boston Massacre when British troops, fired upon a group—of civilian protesters

   C) Boston Massacre, when British troops, fired upon a group of civilian protesters

   D) Boston Massacre—when British troops fired upon a group of civilian protesters

9. A) NO CHANGE

   B) increase

   C) increased

   D) have been increasing

10. Which of the following would be the most appropriate conclusion for the passage?

   A) NO CHANGE

   B) Revere's service to the cause of independence was greater than Dawes's or Prescott's, as shown by the famous poem by Longfellow.

   C) It remains unclear how Revere's service to the cause of independence furthered the movement.

   D) The famous poem by Longfellow expresses the totality of Revere's experience in the Revolutionary War.

the cause of independence certainly does not need a poem in order to be admired. [11]

11. Which of the following provides the strongest supporting evidence for the main claim of the final paragraph?

A) Revere's engraving of the Boston Massacre is displayed in the National Gallery in Washington, D.C.

B) Once hostilities commenced between the British and the revolutionaries, Revere turned his workshop into a gunpowder factory.

C) After the war, Revere opened an iron foundry in Boston.

D) Over the course of the war, Revere proved himself to be one of the bravest supporters of the revolutionary cause.

ANSWERS & EXPLANATIONS

1. A
2. C
3. C
4. B
5. C
6. D
7. C
8. A
9. C
10. A
11. B

1. A
Difficulty: Medium

Category: Writing & Language / Effective Language Use

Strategic Advice: Read the sentences surrounding the underlined word to understand the context. Then, test each answer choice by reading it into the sentence.

Getting to the Answer: The context clues "long been venerated" and "famous" indicate that the answer will be related to fame and glory. "Immortalized" is the best fit for this context. Choice (A) is correct.

2. C
Difficulty: Medium

Category: Writing & Language / Sentence Formation

Strategic Advice: First, read the sentences before and after the period to determine whether they are complete sentences. If they aren't, review the answer choices to find the punctuation needed to join the two grammatical structures.

Getting to the Answer: The grammatical structure after the period is a fragment, and must be joined to the previous sentence. Because the fragment contains information that is not essential to the fundamental meaning of the sentence, it should be set off by a comma. Choice (C) is correct.

3. C
Difficulty: Easy

Category: Writing & Language / Usage

Strategic Advice: Find the pronoun's antecedent and determine the person and number of the antecedent to see which answer choice matches it best. You may need to read the sentence preceding the sentence with the underlined word to find the antecedent.

Getting to the Answer: The pronoun's antecedent is "Revere," which is singular and masculine. Therefore, the pronoun "his" is appropriate here, making (C) correct.

4. B
Difficulty: Hard

Category: Writing & Language / Effective Language Use

Strategic Advice: Look for context clues to establish how the word is used in the sentence. Then, test each choice to find the word that best conveys the author's intended meaning.

Getting to the Answer: The context clues "escaped" and "taken into custody" tell you that the men were arrested, or "apprehended." Choice (B) is correct.

5. C

Difficulty: Hard

Category: Writing & Language / Organization

Strategic Advice: Read the paragraph, paying attention to whether each sentence flows logically into the next. Test each answer choice to see if the change produces a more logical flow of ideas.

Getting to the Answer: The paragraph would flow most logically if sentence 7 were placed directly after sentence 4 because it makes sense to explain that Revere had to return to Lexington on foot before making the statement that he failed in his mission. Choice (C) is correct.

6. D

Difficulty: Hard

Category: Writing & Language / Organization

Strategic Advice: Read the sentence and think about its relationship to the previous sentence. Choose the transitional word or phrase that best shows this relationship.

Getting to the Answer: The second sentence builds upon the first by making a stronger statement. "In fact" indicates that the next sentence will provide an intensification of the first sentence. Therefore, (D) is correct.

7. C

Difficulty: Hard

Category: Writing & Language / Sentence Formation

Strategic Advice: Read the entire sentence containing the underlined portion. Make sure the modifying phrases in the underlined portion are correctly placed.

Getting to the Answer: The modifier "while distinguishing himself as a leading silversmith

of the colonial era" describes Revere, and should be placed as close to his name as possible, (C).

8. A

Difficulty: Medium

Category: Writing & Language / Punctuation

Strategic Advice: Read the entire sentence to determine the relationship of the words on either side of the comma. Then read the underlined portion of the sentence to determine if the punctuation has been placed correctly. Watch out for punctuation that indicates sharp breaks in thought when there are none.

Getting to the Answer: "When British troops . . ." is a nonessential clause modifying "Boston Massacre." A comma is needed to separate a nonessential clause from the rest of the sentence. No other punctuation is needed in the underlined portion of the sentence, so the underlined portion is correct as written. Choice (A) is correct.

9. C

Difficulty: Medium

Category: Writing & Language / Shifts in Construction

Strategic Advice: Read the sentences to look for clues that will tell you what verb tense to use in the underlined portion of the sentence. Clues include dates, time periods, and the tenses of other verbs in the sentence.

Getting to the Answer: The sentence tells you that it takes place in the 1770s, which is a clue that the answer will be the past tense. The other verb in the sentence, "immersed," is in the simple past tense. The answer choice that matches the simple past tense is "increased." Therefore, the correct answer is (C).

10. A

Difficulty: Hard

Category: Writing & Language / Development

Strategic Advice: A concluding sentence should ideally sum up the main idea of the passage. Summarize the main idea of the overall passage in your own words and select the answer choice that best matches your summary.

Getting to the Answer: The passage debunks the notion that Paul Revere's accomplishments were confined to what is described in the poem. Instead, it asserts that his accomplishments are far more extensive. Choice (A) expresses the main idea most clearly and is correct.

11. B

Difficulty: Medium

Category: Writing & Language / Development

Strategic Advice: Identify the main claim of the paragraph and select the answer choice that provides the strongest evidence for that claim. Watch out for answer choices that express opinions, rather than facts.

Getting to the Answer: The main claim of the paragraph is that Revere's contributions to the Revolutionary cause went far beyond the events described in the poem. Choice (B) provides evidence that this is true, and is the correct answer.

The Essay Test

The Kaplan Method for the SAT Essay

The SAT Essay, while optional, presents you with a challenge: to read and understand a high-quality source text and write an essay analyzing the author's argument in 50 minutes. By using the Kaplan Method for the SAT Essay, you will be able to make the most out of those 50 minutes and produce a high-scoring written response to a previously published, sophisticated source.

The Kaplan Method for the SAT Essay consists of four steps:

Step 1: Read the source text, taking notes on how the author uses:

- evidence to support claims
- reasoning to develop ideas and to connect claims and evidence
- stylistic or persuasive elements to add power to the ideas expressed

Step 2: Develop an outline of the features you will analyze in your response

Step 3: Write your essay

Step 4: Check your essay for mistakes in grammar, spelling, and clarity

Step 1: Read the source text, taking notes on how the author uses:

- **evidence to support claims**
- **reasoning to develop ideas and to connect claims and evidence**
- **stylistic or persuasive elements to add power to the ideas expressed**

The source text for the SAT essay will consist of a passage that is very similar to the passages you'll see in the Reading Test. It will typically be 500–750 words and will deal with topics of general interest in the arts, sciences, and public life. In many cases, the passages will be biased in favor of the author's argument.

While the source text changes from test to test, the directions and essay prompt remain similar. Spend more time reading and understanding the text—the prompt will likely be very similar to other prompts that you've encountered.

The notes you take while reading the source text are similar to those you would take when creating a Passage Map on the Reading Test. However, these notes will focus on how the author connects central ideas and important details.

Your notes should focus on:

- evidence to support claims (e.g., cited data or statistics, or authoritative sources that support the author's argument)

- reasoning to develop ideas and make connections (e.g., the author explains his logic for using a specific piece of evidence to support a specific claim)

- stylistic or persuasive elements to add power to the ideas expressed (e.g., using figurative language, irony, metaphor, and other elements to appeal to emotions)

In addition to taking notes in the margins of the passage, it is also helpful to underline and circle the following:

- central ideas

- important details

- facts and opinions

- textual evidence (quotations, paraphrases, or both)

You should spend approximately 10 minutes on Step 1.

Step 2: Develop an outline of the features you will analyze in your response

Creating an outline before you write your essay is a huge time-saver, which is essential when you have only 50 minutes to complete the SAT Essay Test. Spending the first part of the allotted time effectively (i.e., reading and taking notes on the source text and creating an outline) will lead to a well-organized, more convincing essay. You'll also find that organizing your thoughts ahead of time will enable you to write much more quickly!

You should spend approximately 8 minutes on Step 2.

Step 3: Write your essay

After you have read and analyzed the source text and outlined your response, your next goal is to write a cohesive essay that demonstrates your use and command of standard written English. To demonstrate your proficiency, you must:

- Provide your own precise central claim

- Use a variety of sentence structures

- Employ precise word choice

- Maintain a constant and appropriate style and tone

You should spend approximately 30 minutes on Step 3.

Step 4: Check your essay for mistakes in grammar, spelling, and clarity

While a few grammar and spelling mistakes won't drastically harm your SAT Essay score, setting aside some time to proofread can help you catch careless errors that you can easily correct, thereby increasing your Writing score on the SAT Essay.

You should spend the remaining 2 minutes on Step 4.

The SAT Essay Scoring Rubric

There are three different scores for the SAT Essay: Reading, Analysis, and Writing. Each category will be scored on a scale of 1 to 4. The scores you receive will range from 2 to 8, as they will be the scores of two graders.

The graders will use the following rubric to determine each area score.

	1	2
Reading	• Demonstrates **little or no comprehension** of the source text • Fails to show an understanding of the text's central idea(s), and may include only details without reference to central idea(s) • May contain numerous errors of fact and/or interpretation with regard to the text • Makes little or no use of textual evidence	• Demonstrates **some comprehension** of the source text • Shows an understanding of the text's central idea(s) but not of important details • May contain errors of fact and/or interpretation with regard to the text • Makes limited and/or haphazard use of textual evidence
Analysis	• Offers **little or no analysis or ineffective analysis** of the source text and demonstrates **little to no understanding** of the analytical task • Identifies without explanation some aspects of the author's use of evidence, reasoning, and/or stylistic and persuasive elements, and/or feature(s) of the student's own choosing • Numerous aspects of analysis are unwarranted based on the text • Contains little or no support for claim(s) or point(s) made, or support is largely irrelevant • May not focus on features of the text that are relevant to addressing the task • Offers no discernible analysis (e.g., is largely or exclusively summary)	• Offers **limited analysis** of the source text and demonstrates only **partial understanding** of the analytical task • Identifies and attempts to describe the author's use of evidence, reasoning, and/or stylistic and persuasive elements, and/or feature(s) of the student's own choosing, but merely asserts rather than explains their importance • One or more aspects of analysis are unwarranted based on the text • Contains little or no support for claim(s) or point(s) made • May lack a clear focus on those features of the text that are most relevant to addressing the task
Writing	• Demonstrates **little or no cohesion** and **inadequate skill** in the use and control of language • May lack a clear central claim or controlling idea • Lacks a recognizable introduction and conclusion; does not have a discernible progression of ideas • Lacks variety in sentence structures; sentence structures may be repetitive; demonstrates general and vague word choice; word choice may be poor or inaccurate; may lack a formal style and objective tone • Shows a weak control of the conventions of standard written English and may contain numerous errors that undermine the quality of writing	• Demonstrates **little or no cohesion** and **limited skill** in the use and control of language • May lack a clear central claim or controlling idea or may deviate from the claim or idea • May include an ineffective introduction and/or conclusion; may demonstrate some progression of ideas within paragraphs but not throughout • Has limited variety in sentence structures; sentence structures may be repetitive; demonstrates general or vague word choice; word choice may be repetitive; may deviate noticeably from a formal style and objective tone • Shows a limited control of the conventions of standard written English and contains errors that detract from the quality of writing and may impede understanding

	3	4
Reading	• Demonstrates **effective comprehension** of the source text • Shows an understanding of the text's central idea(s) and important details • Is free of substantive errors of fact and interpretation with regard to the text • Makes appropriate use of textual evidence	• Demonstrates **thorough comprehension** of the source text • Shows an understanding of the text's central idea(s) and most important details and how they interrelate • Is free of errors of fact or interpretation with regard to the text • Makes skillful use of textual evidence
Analysis	• Offers an **effective analysis** of the source text and demonstrates an **understanding** of the analytical task • Competently evaluates the author's use of evidence, reasoning, and/or stylistic and persuasive elements, and/or feature(s) of the student's own choosing • Contains relevant and sufficient support for claim(s) or point(s) made • Focuses primarily on those features of the text that are most relevant to addressing the task	• Offers an **insightful analysis** of the source text and demonstrates a **sophisticated understanding** of the analytical task • Offers a thorough, well-considered evaluation of the author's use of evidence, reasoning, and/or stylistic and persuasive elements, and/or feature(s) of the student's own choosing • Contains relevant, sufficient, and strategically chosen support for claim(s) or point(s) made • Focuses consistently on those features of the text that are most relevant to addressing the task
Writing	• Is **mostly cohesive** and demonstrates **effective use and control** of language • Includes a central claim or implicit controlling idea • Includes an effective introduction and conclusion; demonstrates a clear progression of ideas both within paragraphs and throughout the essay • Has variety in sentence structures; demonstrates some precise word choice; maintains a formal style and objective tone • Shows a good control of the conventions of standard written English and is free of significant errors that detract from the quality of writing	• Is **cohesive** and demonstrates a **highly effective use and command** of language • Includes a precise central claim • Includes a skillful introduction and conclusion; demonstrates a deliberate and highly effective progression of ideas both within paragraphs and throughout the essay • Has a wide variety of sentence structures; demonstrates a consistent use of precise word choice; maintains a formal style and objective tone • Shows a strong command of the conventions of standard written English and is free or virtually free of errors

ESSAY PRACTICE SET 1

As you read the passage below, consider how President Kennedy uses

- evidence, such as facts or examples, to support claims.

- reasoning to develop ideas and to connect claims and evidence.

- stylistic or persuasive elements, such as word choice or appeals to emotion, to add power to the ideas expressed.

Adapted from John F. Kennedy's 1961 Inaugural Address.

Vice President Johnson, Mr. Speaker, Mr. Chief Justice, President Eisenhower, Vice President Nixon, President Truman, reverend clergy, fellow citizens, we observe today not a victory of party, but a celebration of freedom—symbolizing an end, as well as a beginning—signifying renewal, as well as change.

Let every nation know, whether it wishes us well or ill, that we shall pay any price, bear any burden, meet any hardship, support any friend, oppose any foe, in order to assure the survival and the success of liberty.

To those nations who would make themselves our adversary, we offer not a pledge but a request: that both sides begin anew the quest for peace, before the dark powers of destruction unleashed by science engulf all humanity in planned or accidental self-destruction.

We dare not tempt them with weakness. For only when our arms are sufficient beyond doubt can we be certain beyond doubt that they will never be employed.

So let us begin anew—remembering on both sides that civility is not a sign of weakness, and sincerity is always subject to proof. Let us never negotiate out of fear. But let us never fear to negotiate.

Let both sides explore what problems unite us instead of belaboring those problems which divide us.

Let both sides, for the first time, formulate serious and precise proposals for the inspection and control of arms—and bring the absolute power to destroy other nations under the absolute control of all nations.

Let both sides seek to invoke the wonders of science instead of its terrors. Together let us explore the stars, conquer the deserts, eradicate disease, tap the ocean depths, and encourage the arts and commerce.

Let both sides unite to heed in all corners of the earth the command of Isaiah—to "undo the heavy burdens ... and to let the oppressed go free."

And if a beachhead of cooperation may push back the jungle of suspicion, let both sides join in creating a new endeavor, not a new balance of power, but a new world of law, where the strong are just and the weak secure and the peace preserved.

All this will not be finished in the first 100 days. Nor will it be finished in the first 1,000 days, nor in the life of this Administration, nor even perhaps in our lifetime on this planet. But let us begin.

In your hands, my fellow citizens, more than in mine, will rest the final success or failure of our course. Since this country was founded, each generation of Americans has been summoned to give testimony to its national loyalty. The graves of young Americans who answered the call to service surround the globe.

Now the trumpet summons us again—not as a call to bear arms, though arms we need; not as a call to battle, though embattled we are—but a call to bear the burden of a long twilight struggle, year in and year out, "rejoicing in hope, patient in tribulation"—a struggle against the common enemies of man: tyranny, poverty, disease, and war itself.

Can we forge against these enemies a grand and global alliance, North and South, East and West, that can assure a more fruitful life for all mankind? Will you join in that historic effort?

In the long history of the world, only a few generations have been granted the role of defending freedom in its hour of maximum danger. I do not shank from this responsibility—I welcome it. I do not believe that any of us would exchange places with any other people or any other generation. The energy, the faith, the devotion which we bring to this endeavor will light our country and all who serve it—and the glow from that fire can truly light the world.

And so, my fellow Americans: ask not what your country can do for you—ask what you can do for your country.

My fellow citizens of the world: ask not what America will do for you, but what together we can do for the freedom of man.

Write an essay in which you explain how President Kennedy builds an argument to persuade his audience that the United States should focus not on developing superior weaponry, but on maintaining peaceful international relations. In your essay, analyze how President Kennedy uses one or more of the features listed previously (or features of your own choice) to strengthen the logic and persuasiveness of his argument. Be sure your analysis focuses on the most relevant aspects of the passage.

Your essay should not explain whether you agree with President Kennedy's claims, but rather explain how President Kennedy builds an argument to persuade his audience.

SAMPLE STUDENT RESPONSE #1

The most famous line from President Kennedy's Inaugural address in January of 1961 is, "ask not what your country can do for you—ask what you can do for your country." But it is the last line of his speech, "ask not what America will do for you, but what together we can do for the freedom of man," that is the underlying theme of his speech: worldwide unity. President Kennedy uses several different methods to get his message of unity across to everyone who was listening: repetition of key phrases and grammatical structures, vivid imagery, and appeals to his audience's sense of duty. Each method is effective in its own way.

Kennedy wanted the world to come together to fight a common enemy: the threat of nuclear war. He uses strong imagery to invoke the horror of nuclear weapons, asking the world to work together "before the dark powers of destruction unleashed by science engulf all humanity in planned or accidental self-destruction." The images suggested by words like "unleashed" and "engulf" convey the urgency of Kennedy's message, driving home the point that countries must act now to avoid total annihilation. Later in the speech, he uses imagery again when he describes a "beachhead of cooperation" that "may push back the jungle of suspicion." By using the contrasting images of a beachhead and a jungle, Kennedy makes cooperation sound more appealing than the climate of suspicion that prevailed at that time. Finally, toward the end of the speech, Kennedy uses imagery that is purely positive as a way of inspiring his audience. He says that the energy, faith and devotion of Americans will "light our country" and "the glow from that fire can truly light the world." This is an effective way of ending the speech on a positive note.

Repetition plays an important part in Kennedy's speech, adding to its power. A phrase Kennedy repeats several times in his speech is "Let both sides." When he lists what he wants out of a united world, he begins with that phrase. Be it stopping nuclear weapons, having the strength to negotiate amongst each other, or asking for simple civility, it is offered under the guide of "both sides." Kennedy didn't want America to act alone. He knew the world would be a dangerous place if no one else came to the table with America to fight against evil. The repetition of the phrase emphasizes the importance of working together to solve the world's problems.

Kennedy also repeats grammatical structures, which helps to build the power of his message. When he says that we must "pay any price, bear any burden, meet any hardship, support any friend, oppose any foe," the repetition of the parallel structures draws the listener's attention in the same way that lyrics in a song capture the imagination. It is both poetic and forceful. He does this again in an inspirational way when he urges the listeners to join with him to "explore the stars, conquer the deserts, eradicate disease, tap the ocean depths." Repetition ensures that listeners will be more likely to remember Kennedy's message, as well.

Kennedy wanted people around the world to come together in the effort to build a more peaceful society. To unite them, he appeals to their sense of duty to fight "a struggle against the common enemies of man." Those common enemies, he said, were "tyranny, poverty, disease, and war itself." By speaking about the necessity of solving common, real-world problems, he was able to show the world that America wants the same thing as everyone else, which is peace and prosperity. He makes the importance of answering this call to duty clear by suggesting the consequences of not acting, as when he speaks about the danger of the "absolute power to destroy other nations."

President Kennedy makes this call of duty even stronger when he invokes the brave soldiers of the past who died in the cause of freedom. He proclaims that the struggle for peace has been a part of every generation, and that "the trumpet summons us" to fight again. But he makes it clear that the freedom and peace that America and its allies sought may not be seen by anyone in the current, or even the next, generation. All he was asking for was for people to answer the call together.

President Kennedy's speech was much more than an address to the nation describing what he was planning to do with his presidency. He used the moment as a platform to speak to the world and let them know that unity is the only way forward. Through calls to duty, evocative imagery, and repetition, he makes his points. He carries these techniques through to the last lines of the speech: first, by saying to America, "ask what you can do for your country." Then, to the world, ask "what together we can do for the freedom of man."

This response scored a 4/4/4

Reading—4: The writer demonstrates a strong ability to comprehend the central ideas and important details of Kennedy's speech, and correctly and effectively uses evidence from the source text in the essay. The essay is free of errors of fact or interpretation.

Analysis—4: The writer clearly understands the analytical task and offers an insightful analysis of the source text. The writer's evaluation of Kennedy's use of rhetorical techniques makes ample use of relevant support from the source text.

Writing—4: The writer makes a strong central claim and employs an effective organization with an introduction, conclusion, and a clear progression of ideas. The essay is cohesive and the writer shows a strong command of the conventions of standard written English so that the essay is virtually free of errors.

SAMPLE STUDENT RESPONSE #2

President Kennedy wanted the world to work together to fight a common enemy. First, he evoked nuclear weapons, asking the world to work together "before the dark powers of destruction unleashed by science engulf all humanity." He goes further mentioning issues that affect everyone everwhere, or, as he put it, "a struggle against the common enemies of man." Those common enemies, he said, were "tyranny, poverty, disease, and war itself." By using real world problems, he was able to show the world that America wants same thing as everyone else, which is peace and prosperity.

Kennedy suggests the consequenses of not acting. For example: when he speaks of nuclear weapons, he says, "We dared not tempt them with weakness." He offers a solution to the problem: … when our arms are suffcient beyond doubt can we be certain beyond doubt that they will never be employed.

Kennedy said we should destroy enemies who wish to do harm with nuclear weapons. That is to make sure that those who are united against such enemies have the firepower needed to ensure that no one ever nuclear weapons again.

He offers hope by calling for "proposals for the inspecion and control of arms—and bring the absolute power to destroy other nations under the absolute control of all nations." Kennedy wanted to make sure that his allies did not think America was looking to control the world, he wanted every nation to take part in keeping the world safe. He finished by asking the world to turn a negative into a positive: "Let both sides seek to invoke the wonders of science instead of its terrors."

President Kennedy left nothing to chance in his address. He mentions several times that the past was the past, and what lay ahead for the future was "renewal," and "symbolizing change."

A phrase Kennedy repeat several times in his speech was "Let both sides." When he listed what he wanted out of a united world, he began with that phrase. Be it stopping nuclear weapons, having the strength to negotiate each other or asking for people to be nicer to each other, it was offered under the guide of "both sides." Kennedy didn't want America to act alone. He knew the world would be a dangerous place if no one else came to the table with America to fight against evil.

This response scored a 2/2/2

Reading—2: The writer demonstrates some comprehension of the central ideas of Kennedy's speech, but shows gaps in understanding. The writer makes limited and haphazard use of textual evidence. The essay shows a lack of clarity in the writer's interpretation of the essay.

Analysis—2: The writer demonstrates only partial understanding of the analytical task and a limited ability to evaluate Kennedy's use of rhetorical techniques. At least one aspect of analysis is unwarranted based on the text, and the essay lacks a clear focus on relevant features of the source text.

Writing—2: The essay demonstrates little cohesion and limited skill in the use and control of language. The essay lacks a coherent introduction and conclusion, and does not show a clear progression of ideas. The writer shows a limited command of the conventions of standard written English, resulting in multiple errors.

ESSAY PRACTICE SET 2

As you read the following passage, consider how Albert Einstein uses

- evidence, such as facts or examples, to support claims.

- reasoning to develop ideas and to connect claims and evidence.

- stylistic or persuasive elements, such as word choice or appeals to emotion, to add power to the ideas expressed.

Adapted from Albert Einstein's speech "Peace in the Atomic Era," which he delivered at Princeton University on February 19, 1950.

I am grateful to you for the opportunity to express my conviction in this most important political question.

The idea of achieving security through national armament is, at the present state of military technique, a disastrous illusion. On the part of the United States this illusion has been particularly fostered by the fact that this country succeeded first in producing an atomic bomb. The belief seemed to prevail that in the end it were possible to achieve decisive military superiority.

In this way, any potential opponent would be intimidated, and security, so ardently desired by all of us, brought to us and all of humanity. The maxim which we have been following during these last five years has been, in short: security through superior military power, whatever the cost.

This mechanistic, technical-military psychological attitude had inevitable consequences. Every single act in foreign policy is governed exclusively by one viewpoint. How do we have to act in order to achieve utmost superiority over the opponent in case of war? Establishing military bases at all possible strategically important points on the globe. Arming and economic strengthening of potential allies.

Within the country—concentration of tremendous financial power in the hands of the military, militarization of the youth, close supervision of the loyalty of the citizens, in particular, of the civil servants by a police force growing more conspicuous every day. Intimidation of people of independent political thinking. Indoctrination of the public by radio, press, school. Growing restriction of the range of public information under the pressure of military secrecy.

The armament race between the U.S.A. and the U.S.S.R., originally supposed to be a preventive measure, assumes hysterical character. On both sides, the means to mass destruction are perfected with feverish haste—behind the respective walls of secrecy. The H-bomb appears on the public horizon as a probably attainable goal. Its accelerated development has been solemnly proclaimed by the President.

If successful, radioactive poisoning of the atmosphere and hence annihilation of any life on earth has been brought within the range of technical possibilities. The ghostlike character of this development lies in its apparently compulsory trend. Every step appears as the unavoidable consequence of the preceding one. In the end, there beckons more and more clearly general annihilation.

Is there any way out of this impasse created by man himself? All of us, and particularly those who are responsible for the attitude of the U.S. and the U.S.S.R., should realize that we may have vanquished an external enemy, but have been incapable of getting rid of the mentality created by the war.

It is impossible to achieve peace as long as every single action is taken with a possible future conflict in view. The leading point of view of all political action should therefore be: What can we do to bring about a peaceful co-existence and even loyal cooperation of the nations?

The first problem is to do away with mutual fear and distrust. Solemn renunciation of violence (not only with respect to means of mass destruction) is undoubtedly necessary.

Such renunciation, however, can only be effective if at the same time a supra-national judicial and executive body is set up empowered to decide questions of immediate concern to the security of the nations. Even a declaration of the nations to collaborate loyally in the realization of such a "restricted world government" would considerably reduce the imminent danger of war.

In the last analysis, every kind of peaceful cooperation among men is primarily based on mutual trust and only secondly on institutions such as courts of justice and police. This holds for nations as well as for individuals. And the basis of trust is loyal give and take.

What about international control? Well, it may be of secondary use as a police measure. But it may be wise to overestimate its importance. The times of prohibition come to mind and give one pause.

Write an essay in which you explain how Einstein builds an argument to persuade his audience that worldwide peace can be achieved only through cooperation. In your essay, analyze how Einstein uses one or more of the features listed previously (or features of your own choice) to strengthen the logic and persuasiveness of his argument. Be sure your analysis focuses on the most relevant aspects of the passage.

Your essay should not explain whether you agree with Einstein's claims, but rather explain how Einstein builds an argument to persuade his audience.

SAMPLE STUDENT RESPONSE #1

Albert Einstein believed that worldwide peace can only be achieved through the cooperation of nations. His speech is constructed to present the horrors of nuclear annhilation first, followed by a presentation of solutions. He also effectively uses logical reasoning and evidence to build his argument and support his points.

Einstein begins his argument for worldwide peace not by pointing out the positive aspects of peace, but instead describing what the world would be like if the world continued down the path of war and nuclear destruction. His speech metaphoricaly digs a hole and makes it look like the world would never be able to climb out of it. He then offered solutions to the dire problems he presented, giving the world the tools necessary to fill the metaphorical hole back up.

Einstein doesn't mince words when he begins. He calls "security through national armament" a "disastrous illusion." He supports this claim with the evidence of America creating the first atomic bomb. Einstein states that this acheivement was the basis of the "illusion" that America would be able to achieve peace through "military superiority." In other words, since America had the "bomb," they would be able to keep every other nation in check. Einstein stops short of calling America arrogant, but the implication is clear when he states, "any potential opponent would be intimidated, and security, so ardently desired by all of us, brought to us and all of humanity . . . in short: security through superior military power, whatever the cost."

Einstein delves into what the "inevitable consequences" or "cost" was. First discussing the ways "superior military power" was displayed worldwide—putting military bases around the world, arming America's allies. He then brings up the consequences within America of using such power: "tremendous financial power in the hands of the military, militarization of the youth, close supervision of the loyalty of the citizens," as well as "growing restriction of the range of public information under the pressure of military secrecy." The evidence he presents helps to prove his point that a militaristic attitude has led America down the wrong path.

Einstein paints an even bleaker picture when he discusses the arms race between America and the U.S.S.R. He presents evidence of the "hysteria" of this race, with each nation plotting to be the strongest military presence in the world "behind the respective walls of secrecy." He goes further when he brings up the possibility of the H-bomb. He reasons that "if successful," Einstein says, "radioactive poisoning of the atmosphere and hence annihlation of any life on earth has been brought within the range of technical possibilities." Einstein completes the thought by saying that each dangerous choice America and the U.S.S.R. creates the "unavoidable consequence of the preceding one. In the end, there beckons more and more clearly general annihlation." Einstein's reasoning and evidence work together to make his points.

The effectiveness of the structure of the speech become clear again later when after scaring the country with the future of the world on its current path Einstein creates an alternative path by asking, "Is there any way out of this impasse created by man himself?" Einstein appears to believe the answer is "yes," but the path will not be easy.

He states that mistrust and fear of each other must stop. Next, military-type countries must have a "solemn renunciation of violence." But this renunciation "can only be effective if" countries created an outside judicial body. Einstein even believes that a simple "declaration of the nations to collaborate loyally . . . would considerably reduce the imminent danger of war."

By first laying out the cost of runaway military might, he makes it easier to introduce solutions that nations may otherwise ignore. Einstein gave America and the world a glimpse of what could be both positive and negative and he wisely ended his speech with the positive, leaving everyone with the knowledge that war is not necessarily inevitable. And, if countries work together and trust each other true peace can be acheived.

This response scored a 4/3/3

Reading—4: The writer demonstrates a strong ability to comprehend the central ideas and important details of Einstein's speech, and correctly and effectively uses evidence from the source text in the essay. The essay is free of errors of fact or interpretation.

Analysis—3: The writer demonstrates an understanding of the analytical task and offers an effective analysis of the source text. The writer's evaluation of Einstein's use of rhetorical techniques makes sufficient use of relevant support from the source text.

Writing—3: The essay demonstrates sufficient skill in the use and control of language. The essay includes an effective introduction and conclusion, and shows a clear progression of ideas. The writer demonstrates sufficient command of the conventions of standard written English, with errors that do not detract significantly from the effectiveness of the argument.

SAMPLE STUDENT RESPONSE #2

Einstein wanted peace. He did not want war. I agree that nucleur war shoud be avoided all costs, we shoud not try to make more weapons than other countrys do. Einstein said 'In this way, any potential opponent would be initmdated.' He meant this was not a good thing. Einstein was a peaceful man.

He did not trust the military and he thought the youth were too military. He thought citizens were not loyal to the military. He supported 'restriction of the range of public information under the pressure of military secrety.'

The USA/USSR disagreement was hysteria to Einstein. He thought there were to many secrets about the H bomb and the "acelerated development has been solemnly proclaimed by the president."

Einsten wanted to acheve peace. He was against war. He wanted rennunciation and international control and I agree with him.

This response scored a 1/1/1

Reading—1: The writer demonstrates little to no comprehension of Einstein's speech and fails to show an understanding of the text's central ideas. The essay contains numerous errors of fact and interpretation of the source text. The writer makes ineffective use of textual evidence.

Analysis—1: The writer demonstrates a lack of understanding of the analytical task and offers incorrect analysis of the source text. The writer shows an inability to focus on the relevant features of the source text.

Writing—1: The writer demonstrates little ability to provide a central claim, organization, or progression of ideas. The writer uses repetitive sentence structures and fails to show command of the conventions of standard written English, resulting in numerous errors that undermine the quality of the writing.

ESSAY PRACTICE SET 3

As you read the following passage, consider how Winston Churchill uses

- evidence, such as facts or examples, to support claims.

- reasoning to develop ideas and to connect claims and evidence.

- stylistic or persuasive elements, such as word choice or appeals to emotion, to add power to the ideas expressed.

Adapted from Winston Churchill's first speech as British Prime Minister to the House of Commons of the Parliament of the United Kingdom on May 13, 1940.

On Friday evening last I received from His Majesty the mission to form a new administration. It was the evident will of Parliament and the nation that this should be conceived on the broadest possible basis and that it should include all parties.

I have already completed the most important part of this task.

A war cabinet has been formed of five members, representing, with the Labour, Opposition, and Liberals, the unity of the nation. It was necessary that this should be done in one single day on account of the extreme urgency and rigor of events. Other key positions were filled yesterday. I am submitting a further list to the king tonight. I hope to complete the appointment of principal ministers during tomorrow.

The appointment of other ministers usually takes a little longer. I trust when Parliament meets again this part of my task will be completed and that the administration will be complete in all respects. I considered it in the public interest to suggest to the Speaker that the House should be summoned today.

At the end of today's proceedings, the adjournment of the House will be proposed until May 21 with provision for earlier meeting if need be. Business for that will be notified to MPs at the earliest opportunity.

I now invite the House by a resolution to record its approval of the steps taken and declare its confidence in the new government.

The resolution:

"That this House welcomes the formation of a government representing the united and inflexible resolve of the nation to prosecute the war with Germany to a victorious conclusion."

To form an administration of this scale and complexity is a serious undertaking in itself. But we are in the preliminary phase of one of the greatest battles in history. We are in action at many other points—in Norway and in Holland—and we have to be prepared in the Mediterranean. The air battle is continuing, and many preparations have to be made here at home.

In this crisis I think I may be pardoned if I do not address the House at any length today, and I hope that any of my friends and colleagues or former colleagues who are affected by the political reconstruction will make all allowances for any lack of ceremony with which it has been necessary to act.

I say to the House as I said to ministers who have joined this government, I have nothing to offer but blood, toil, tears, and sweat. We have before us an ordeal of the most grievous kind. We have before us many, many months of struggle and suffering.

You ask, what is our policy? I say it is to wage war by land, sea, and air. War with all our might and with all the strength God has given us, and to wage war against a monstrous tyranny never surpassed in the dark and lamentable catalogue of human crime. That is our policy.

You ask, what is our aim? I can answer in one word. It is victory. Victory at all costs—Victory in spite of all terrors—Victory, however long and hard the road may be, for without victory there is no survival.

Let that be realized. No survival for the British Empire, no survival for all that the British Empire has stood for, no survival for the urge, the impulse of the ages, that mankind shall move forward toward his goal.

I take up my task in buoyancy and hope. I feel sure that our cause will not be suffered to fail among men. I feel entitled at this juncture, at this time, to claim the aid of all and to say, "Come then, let us go forward together with our united strength."

Write an essay in which you explain how Churchill builds an argument to persuade his audience that the British should keep fighting in World War II, even if the enemy seems invincible. In your essay, analyze how Churchill uses one or more of the features listed previously (or features of your own choice) to strengthen the logic and persuasiveness of his argument. Be sure your analysis focuses on the most relevant aspects of the passage.

Your essay should not explain whether you agree with Churchill's claims, but rather explain how Churchill builds an argument to persuade his audience.

SAMPLE STUDENT RESPONSE #1

In 1940, Winston Churchill issued a resolution for Parliament to approve in order for them to show confidence in Churchill and the new administration he created. The resolution stated, "That this House welcomes the formation of a government representing the united and inflexible resolve of the nation to prosecute the war with Germany to a victorious conclusion." To convince Parliament to approve the resolution, Churchill built an argument that the British should keep fighting the Germans with all their might. He built his argument through plainspoken reasoning, rhetorical questions, and inspirational imagery and turns of phrase.

At the beginning of his speech, Churchill does away with pomp and circumstance. He gets right down to business, explaining the ongoing changes in the government. His matter-of-fact tone shows that he is serious about the task at hand. Churchill continues using this businesslike tone to lay out his reasoning for the resolution: "We are in the preliminary phase of one of the greatest battles in history … The air battle is continuing, and many preparations have to be made here at home." His explanation is logical and persuasive, and his tone gives his audience confidence that his focus was solely on winning the war. To emphasize his seriousness about the matter, he adds, "I hope that any of my friends and colleagues … will make all allowances for any lack of ceremony with which it has been necessary to act."

Churchill's plainspoken, almost hard-headed reasoning continues as he paints a bleak picture of Britain's chances in the war. He made it clear that the road ahead was far from easy: "We have before us an ordeal of the most grievous kind. We have before us many, many months of struggle and suffering." He also assured Britain that he was not offering an easy way out, when he said, "I have nothing to offer but blood, toil, tears, and sweat." The implication of this statement was that "blood, toil, tears, and sweat" would be required of every citizen. Churchill used this strong dose of reality to preclude any ideas of a clean, simple victory over Germany. The language is harsh, but it helps to prepare the audience for the stark choices that lay ahead.

At this point in the speech, Churchill knew the people of Britain would have questions about policy, procedure, and maybe even "why are we going to fight this war if we cannot win?" Churchill took this on directly by raising the questions rhetorically: "You ask, what is our policy? I say it is to wage war by land, sea, and air. … You ask, what is our aim? I can answer in one word. It is victory." By asking rhetorical question and then answering them, Churchill crafted his speech as if it were a conversation, which had the effect of drawing the people of Britain together.

Though Churchill answered the questions simply at first, he extrapolated on the brief answers with strong phrasing and imagery to leave the people of Britain with both a compelling reason to fight, and the hope that Britain would be victorious. When he spoke of waging a war "by land, sea, and air," he proclaimed that this three-pronged attack was necessary to "wage war against a monstrous tyranny never surpassed in the dark and lamentable catalogue of human crime." When he spoke of "victory," he declared that Britain would achieve it "at all costs … in spite of all terrors … however long and hard the road may be, for without victory there is no survival." Churchill used the word "victory" several times in that section of the speech, repeating the triumphant word to instill it into the people of Britain.

This type of stirring, inspirational language and imagery contrasts with the businesslike tone at the beginning of the speech, and this is intentional on Churchill's part. After establishing his credibility with simple language at the beginning of the speech, he ends with vibrant, evocative language that will inspire Parliament, and the nation, to act.

To wrap up the speech, Churchill made it clear how he personally felt about Britain's chances when he said, "I take up my task in buoyancy and hope." He then included the people in this positive outlook: "Come then, let us go forward together with our united strength." Churchill began his speech in the darkest of places, and ended the speech in the brightest place possible: a place of hope and victory.

This response scored a 4/4/4

Reading—4: The writer demonstrates a strong ability to comprehend the central ideas and important details of Churchill's speech, and correctly and effectively uses evidence from the source text in the essay. The essay is free of errors of fact or interpretation.

Analysis—4: The writer demonstrates an understanding the analytical task and offers an insightful analysis of the source text. The writer's evaluation of Churchill's use of rhetorical techniques is thorough and well considered, and makes ample use of relevant support from the source text. The writer focuses consistently on the most relevant features of the text.

Writing—4: The writer makes a precise central claim and employs an effective organization with a skillful introduction, conclusion, and a clear progression of ideas. The essay is cohesive and the writer shows a strong command of the conventions of standard written English, resulting in an essay that is virtually free of errors.

SAMPLE STUDENT RESPONSE #2

Winston Churchill was a good man who knew how to convince people of what to think. He understood that the British had to go to war, and he wanted the King to understand that too. That is why he used this speech to convince the King that Churchills ideas were right.

Churchill used strong words like "united" and "inflexible" in his speech. He used these words to show how the British should be strong and fight the Germans. These words helped to sway the King and the public.

"I have nothing to offer but blood, toll, tears, and sweat." Churchill wanted them to know they were all in this together. That is what strong leaders do, tell people that they all have to work together to fight an enemny. They have to give people bad news. Churchill said we have many months of struggle and sufferring. He said this so people who were afraid could know what was coming. Churchil also wanted people to know he was afraid just like them. He was human too.

"You ask, what is our policy? I say it is to wage war by land, sea, and air. War with all our might and with all the strength God has given us, and to wage war against a monstrous tyranny never surpassed in the dark and lamentable catalogue of human crime. That is our policy." He does this to explain his argument.

Churchill built an argument in his speech. He talked about hope. He said finally "come, let us go foward together with our untied strength." this was a strong way to end the speech.

This response scored a 2/1/1

Reading—2: The writer demonstrates inconsistent comprehension of the central ideas and important details of Churchill's speech. The essay contains errors of fact and interpretation with regard to the text. The writer makes limited and haphazard use of textual evidence.

Analysis—1: The writer offers little to no analysis of Churchill's speech and demonstrates only partial understanding of the analytical task. The essay identifies Churchill's use strong words but does not correctly explain the importance. The writer spends more time discussing Churchill's thoughts and beliefs than the argument Churchill makes in the speech, which demonstrates a lack of comprehension of the task.

Writing—1: The essay demonstrates poor organization and little to no skill in the use and control of language. The writer includes an introduction and conclusion, but does not demonstrate an ability to use them effectively, and the essay does not show a clear progression of ideas. The writer's command of the conventions of standard written English is limited, resulting in multiple errors.

SECTION FOUR

Practice Test

HOW TO SCORE YOUR PRACTICE TESTS

For each subject area in the practice test, convert your raw score, or the number of questions you answered correctly, to a scaled score using the following table. To get your raw score for Evidence-Based Reading & Writing, add the total number of Reading questions you answered correctly to the total number of Writing questions you answered correctly.

Evidence-Based Reading and Writing			
TOTAL Raw Score	Scaled Score	TOTAL Raw Score	Scaled Score
0	200	49	490
1	200	50	500
2	210	51	500
3	220	52	510
4	240	53	510
5	260	54	520
6	270	55	520
7	270	56	530
8	290	57	530
9	290	58	540
10	300	59	540
11	300	60	550
12	310	61	550
13	320	62	560
14	320	63	560
15	330	64	570
16	330	65	570
17	340	66	580
18	340	67	580
19	350	68	590
20	350	69	590
21	360	70	600
22	360	71	600
23	370	72	610
24	370	73	610
25	370	74	610
26	380	75	620
27	380	76	620
28	380	77	630
29	380	78	630
30	390	79	640
31	390	80	640
32	400	81	660
33	400	82	660
34	410	83	670
35	410	84	680
36	420	85	690
37	430	86	700
38	430	87	700
39	440	88	710
40	440	89	710
41	450	90	730
42	450	91	740
43	460	92	750
44	460	93	760
45	470	94	780
46	480	95	790
47	480	96	800
48	490		

SAT PRACTICE TEST ANSWER SHEET

Remove (or photocopy) this answer sheet and use it to complete the test. See the answer key following the test when finished.

Start with number 1 for each section. If a section has fewer questions than answer spaces, leave the extra spaces blank.

SECTION 1

1. Ⓐ Ⓑ Ⓒ Ⓓ
2. Ⓐ Ⓑ Ⓒ Ⓓ
3. Ⓐ Ⓑ Ⓒ Ⓓ
4. Ⓐ Ⓑ Ⓒ Ⓓ
5. Ⓐ Ⓑ Ⓒ Ⓓ
6. Ⓐ Ⓑ Ⓒ Ⓓ
7. Ⓐ Ⓑ Ⓒ Ⓓ
8. Ⓐ Ⓑ Ⓒ Ⓓ
9. Ⓐ Ⓑ Ⓒ Ⓓ
10. Ⓐ Ⓑ Ⓒ Ⓓ
11. Ⓐ Ⓑ Ⓒ Ⓓ
12. Ⓐ Ⓑ Ⓒ Ⓓ
13. Ⓐ Ⓑ Ⓒ Ⓓ

14. Ⓐ Ⓑ Ⓒ Ⓓ
15. Ⓐ Ⓑ Ⓒ Ⓓ
16. Ⓐ Ⓑ Ⓒ Ⓓ
17. Ⓐ Ⓑ Ⓒ Ⓓ
18. Ⓐ Ⓑ Ⓒ Ⓓ
19. Ⓐ Ⓑ Ⓒ Ⓓ
20. Ⓐ Ⓑ Ⓒ Ⓓ
21. Ⓐ Ⓑ Ⓒ Ⓓ
22. Ⓐ Ⓑ Ⓒ Ⓓ
23. Ⓐ Ⓑ Ⓒ Ⓓ
24. Ⓐ Ⓑ Ⓒ Ⓓ
25. Ⓐ Ⓑ Ⓒ Ⓓ
26. Ⓐ Ⓑ Ⓒ Ⓓ

27. Ⓐ Ⓑ Ⓒ Ⓓ
28. Ⓐ Ⓑ Ⓒ Ⓓ
29. Ⓐ Ⓑ Ⓒ Ⓓ
30. Ⓐ Ⓑ Ⓒ Ⓓ
31. Ⓐ Ⓑ Ⓒ Ⓓ
32. Ⓐ Ⓑ Ⓒ Ⓓ
33. Ⓐ Ⓑ Ⓒ Ⓓ
34. Ⓐ Ⓑ Ⓒ Ⓓ
35. Ⓐ Ⓑ Ⓒ Ⓓ
36. Ⓐ Ⓑ Ⓒ Ⓓ
37. Ⓐ Ⓑ Ⓒ Ⓓ
38. Ⓐ Ⓑ Ⓒ Ⓓ
39. Ⓐ Ⓑ Ⓒ Ⓓ

40. Ⓐ Ⓑ Ⓒ Ⓓ
41. Ⓐ Ⓑ Ⓒ Ⓓ
42. Ⓐ Ⓑ Ⓒ Ⓓ
43. Ⓐ Ⓑ Ⓒ Ⓓ
44. Ⓐ Ⓑ Ⓒ Ⓓ
45. Ⓐ Ⓑ Ⓒ Ⓓ
46. Ⓐ Ⓑ Ⓒ Ⓓ
47. Ⓐ Ⓑ Ⓒ Ⓓ
48. Ⓐ Ⓑ Ⓒ Ⓓ
49. Ⓐ Ⓑ Ⓒ Ⓓ
50. Ⓐ Ⓑ Ⓒ Ⓓ
51. Ⓐ Ⓑ Ⓒ Ⓓ
52. Ⓐ Ⓑ Ⓒ Ⓓ

☐ # right in Section 1

☐ # wrong in Section 1

SECTION 2

1. Ⓐ Ⓑ Ⓒ Ⓓ
2. Ⓐ Ⓑ Ⓒ Ⓓ
3. Ⓐ Ⓑ Ⓒ Ⓓ
4. Ⓐ Ⓑ Ⓒ Ⓓ
5. Ⓐ Ⓑ Ⓒ Ⓓ
6. Ⓐ Ⓑ Ⓒ Ⓓ
7. Ⓐ Ⓑ Ⓒ Ⓓ
8. Ⓐ Ⓑ Ⓒ Ⓓ
9. Ⓐ Ⓑ Ⓒ Ⓓ
10. Ⓐ Ⓑ Ⓒ Ⓓ
11. Ⓐ Ⓑ Ⓒ Ⓓ

12. Ⓐ Ⓑ Ⓒ Ⓓ
13. Ⓐ Ⓑ Ⓒ Ⓓ
14. Ⓐ Ⓑ Ⓒ Ⓓ
15. Ⓐ Ⓑ Ⓒ Ⓓ
16. Ⓐ Ⓑ Ⓒ Ⓓ
17. Ⓐ Ⓑ Ⓒ Ⓓ
18. Ⓐ Ⓑ Ⓒ Ⓓ
19. Ⓐ Ⓑ Ⓒ Ⓓ
20. Ⓐ Ⓑ Ⓒ Ⓓ
21. Ⓐ Ⓑ Ⓒ Ⓓ
22. Ⓐ Ⓑ Ⓒ Ⓓ

23. Ⓐ Ⓑ Ⓒ Ⓓ
24. Ⓐ Ⓑ Ⓒ Ⓓ
25. Ⓐ Ⓑ Ⓒ Ⓓ
26. Ⓐ Ⓑ Ⓒ Ⓓ
27. Ⓐ Ⓑ Ⓒ Ⓓ
28. Ⓐ Ⓑ Ⓒ Ⓓ
29. Ⓐ Ⓑ Ⓒ Ⓓ
30. Ⓐ Ⓑ Ⓒ Ⓓ
31. Ⓐ Ⓑ Ⓒ Ⓓ
32. Ⓐ Ⓑ Ⓒ Ⓓ
33. Ⓐ Ⓑ Ⓒ Ⓓ

34. Ⓐ Ⓑ Ⓒ Ⓓ
35. Ⓐ Ⓑ Ⓒ Ⓓ
36. Ⓐ Ⓑ Ⓒ Ⓓ
37. Ⓐ Ⓑ Ⓒ Ⓓ
38. Ⓐ Ⓑ Ⓒ Ⓓ
39. Ⓐ Ⓑ Ⓒ Ⓓ
40. Ⓐ Ⓑ Ⓒ Ⓓ
41. Ⓐ Ⓑ Ⓒ Ⓓ
42. Ⓐ Ⓑ Ⓒ Ⓓ
43. Ⓐ Ⓑ Ⓒ Ⓓ
44. Ⓐ Ⓑ Ⓒ Ⓓ

☐ # right in Section 2

☐ # wrong in Section 2

READING TEST

65 Minutes—52 Questions

Turn to Section 1 of your answer sheet to answer the questions in this section.

Directions: Each passage or pair of passages below is followed by a number of questions. After reading each passage or pair, choose the best answer to each question based on what is stated or implied in the passage or passages and in any accompanying graphics (such as a table or graph).

Questions 1-10 are based on the following passage.

The following passage is adapted from Leo Tolstoy's 1873 novel, Anna Karenina *(translated from the original Russian by Constance Garnett). Prior to this excerpt, one of the major characters, Levin, has realized that he is in love with his longtime friend Kitty Shtcherbatsky.*

At four o'clock, conscious of his throbbing heart, Levin stepped out of a hired sledge at the Zoological Gardens, and turned along the path to the frozen
Line mounds and the skating ground, knowing that he
(5) would certainly find her there, as he had seen the Shtcherbatskys' carriage at the entrance.

It was a bright, frosty day. Rows of carriages, sledges, drivers, and policemen were standing in the approach. Crowds of well-dressed people, with hats
(10) bright in the sun, swarmed about the entrance and along the well-swept little paths between the little houses adorned with carving in the Russian style. The old curly birches of the gardens, all their twigs laden with snow, looked as though freshly decked in
(15) sacred vestments.

He walked along the path towards the skating-ground, and kept saying to himself—"You mustn't be excited, you must be calm. What's the matter with you? What do you want? Be quiet, stupid," he
(20) conjured his heart. And the more he tried to compose himself, the more breathless he found himself. An acquaintance met him and called him by his name, but Levin did not even recognize him. He went towards the mounds, whence came the clank
(25) of the chains of sledges as they slipped down or were dragged up, the rumble of the sliding sledges, and the sounds of merry voices. He walked on a few steps, and the skating-ground lay open before his

eyes, and at once, amidst all the skaters, he knew her.
(30) He knew she was there by the rapture and the ter-ror that seized on his heart. She was standing talking to a lady at the opposite end of the ground. There was apparently nothing striking either in her dress or her attitude. But for Levin she was as easy to find
(35) in that crowd as a rose among nettles. Everything was made bright by her. She was the smile that shed light on all round her. "Is it possible I can go over there on the ice, go up to her?" he thought. The place where she stood seemed to him a holy shrine, unap-
(40) proachable, and there was one moment when he was almost retreating, so overwhelmed was he with terror. He had to make an effort to master himself, and to remind himself that people of all sorts were moving about her, and that he too might come there
(45) to skate. He walked down, for a long while avoiding looking at her as at the sun, but seeing her, as one does the sun, without looking.

On that day of the week and at that time of day people of one set, all acquainted with one another,
(50) used to meet on the ice. There were crack skaters there, showing off their skill, and learners clinging to chairs with timid, awkward movements, boys, and elderly people skating with hygienic motives. They seemed to Levin an elect band of blissful beings
(55) because they were here, near her. All the skaters, it seemed, with perfect self-possession, skated towards her, skated by her, even spoke to her, and were happy, quite apart from her, enjoying the capital ice and the fine weather.

(60) Nikolay Shtcherbatsky, Kitty's cousin, in a short jacket and tight trousers, was sitting on a garden seat with his skates on. Seeing Levin, he shouted to him:

GO ON TO THE NEXT PAGE →

"Ah, the first skater in Russia! Been here long?
(65) First-rate ice—do put your skates on."

1. According to the passage, how did Levin first know that Kitty was at the Zoological Gardens?

   A) Kitty's carriage was parked near the entrance.

   B) Nikolay said he had been skating with Kitty earlier.

   C) He saw her talking with another woman near the pond.

   D) Kitty invited him to meet her there at a certain time.

2. As used in line 10, "swarmed" most nearly means

   A) invaded.

   B) gathered.

   C) flew.

   D) obstructed.

3. The passage most strongly suggests that which of the following is true of Levin?

   A) He worries about his appearance.

   B) He wishes he were more impressive.

   C) He is an extremely passionate person.

   D) He is wary of his surroundings.

4. Which choice provides the best evidence for the answer to the previous question?

   A) Lines 7-12 ("It was a bright, frosty day . . . in the Russian style")

   B) Lines 22-27 ("An acquaintance met him . . . merry voices")

   C) Lines 38-45 ("The place where . . . there to skate")

   D) Lines 48-53 ("On that day . . . hygienic motives")

5. What theme does the passage communicate through the experiences of Levin?

   A) Love is a powerful emotion.

   B) People long to have company.

   C) Life should be filled with joy.

   D) People are meant to work hard.

6. The passage most strongly suggests that which of the following is true of how Levin appears to others?

   A) People think that Levin looks agitated because of the way he is acting.

   B) People think that Levin is sick because he seems to be feverish.

   C) People think that Levin seems normal because he is doing nothing unusual.

   D) People think that Levin is in trouble because he is not protecting himself emotionally.

7. Which choice provides the best evidence for the answer to the previous question?

   A) Lines 1-6 ("At four o'clock . . . at the entrance")

   B) Lines 9-12 ("Crowds . . . the Russian style")

   C) Lines 23-29 ("He went . . . he knew her")

   D) Lines 60-65 ("Nikolay Shtcherbatsky . . . your skates on")

8. As used in line 20, "conjured" most nearly means

   A) begged.

   B) created.

   C) summoned.

   D) tricked.

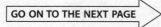
GO ON TO THE NEXT PAGE

9. The author's use of the word "throbbing" in line 1 implies that Levin

   A) has cut himself badly.

   B) has a sudden pain in his chest.

   C) is about to collapse.

   D) is in an agitated state.

10. Based on the tone of this passage, what emotion does the author wish the reader to feel about Levin?

   A) Empathy

   B) Cynicism

   C) Hostility

   D) Disgust

Questions 11-20 are based on the following passage.

This passage is adapted from a speech delivered by President Franklin Roosevelt on January 6, 1941, to the United States Congress. In the passage, Roosevelt reveals his intention to preserve and spread American ideals around the world.

The Nation takes great satisfaction and much strength from the things which have been done to make its people conscious of their individual stake
Line in the preservation of democratic life in America.
(5) Those things have toughened the fibre of our people, have renewed their faith and strengthened their devotion to the institutions we make ready to protect.

Certainly this is no time for any of us to stop thinking about the social and economic problems
(10) which are the root cause of the social revolution which is today a supreme factor in the world.

For there is nothing mysterious about the foundations of a healthy and strong democracy. The basic things expected by our people of their political and
(15) economic systems are simple. They are:

- Equality of opportunity for youth and for others.

- Jobs for those who can work.

- Security for those who need it.

- The ending of special privilege for the few.

(20) • The preservation of civil liberties for all.

• The enjoyment of the fruits of scientific progress in a wider and constantly rising standard of living.

These are the simple, basic things that must never be lost sight of in the turmoil and unbelievable com-
(25) plexity of our modern world. The inner and abiding strength of our economic and political systems is dependent upon the degree to which they fulfill these expectations.

Many subjects connected with our social econo-
(30) my call for immediate improvement.

As examples:

• We should bring more citizens under the coverage of old-age pensions and unemployment insurance.

• We should widen the opportunities for adequate
(35) medical care.

• We should plan a better system by which persons deserving or needing gainful employment may obtain it.

I have called for personal sacrifice. I am as-
(40) sured of the willingness of almost all Americans to respond to that call.

A part of the sacrifice means the payment of more money in taxes. In my Budget Message I shall recommend that a greater portion of this great de-
(45) fense program be paid for from taxation than we are paying today. No person should try, or be allowed, to get rich out of this program; and the principle of tax payments in accordance with ability to pay should be constantly before our eyes to guide our legislation.

(50) If the Congress maintains these principles, the voters, putting patriotism ahead of pocketbooks, will give you their applause.

In the future days, which we seek to make secure, we look forward to a world founded upon four
(55) essential human freedoms.

The first is freedom of speech and expression— everywhere in the world.

The second is freedom of every person to worship God in his own way—everywhere in the world.

(60) The third is freedom from want—which, translated into world terms, means economic

GO ON TO THE NEXT PAGE

understandings which will secure to every nation a healthy peacetime life for its inhabitants—every-where in the world.

(65) The fourth is freedom from fear—which, translated into world terms, means a world-wide reduction of armaments to such a point and in such a thorough fashion that no nation will be in a posi-tion to commit an act of physical aggression against
(70) any neighbor—anywhere in the world.

That is no vision of a distant millennium. It is a definite basis for a kind of world attainable in our own time and generation. That kind of world is the very antithesis of the so-called new order of
(75) tyranny which the dictators seek to create with the crash of a bomb.

To that new order we oppose the greater conception—the moral order. A good society is able to face schemes of world domination and
(80) foreign revolutions alike without fear.

Since the beginning of our American history, we have been engaged in change—in a perpetual peaceful revolution—a revolution which goes on steadily, quietly adjusting itself to changing
(85) conditions—without the concentration camp or the quick-lime in the ditch. The world order which we seek is the cooperation of free countries, working together in a friendly, civilized society.

This nation has placed its destiny in the hands
(90) and heads and hearts of its millions of free men and women; and its faith in freedom under the guid-ance of God. Freedom means the supremacy of hu-man rights everywhere. Our support goes to those who struggle to gain those rights or keep them.
(95) Our strength is our unity of purpose. To that high concept there can be no end save victory.

11. Which phrase from the passage most clearly re-flects President Roosevelt's purpose in making this speech?

A) Lines 2-4 ("to make . . . democratic life")

B) Lines 8-11 ("to stop thinking . . . the world")

C) Lines 54-55 ("[to] look forward to . . . freedoms")

D) Lines 79-80 ("to face . . . without fear")

12. Which choice provides the best evidence for the answer to the previous question?

A) Lines 13-15 ("The basic things . . . are simple")

B) Lines 29-30 ("Many subjects . . . improve-ment")

C) Lines 50-52 ("If the Congress . . . applause")

D) Lines 53-55 ("In the future days . . . freedoms")

13. As used in line 39, "sacrifice" most nearly means

A) religious offerings to a deity.

B) service in the military.

C) losses of limbs in battle.

D) surrender of interests to a greater good.

14. The passage most strongly suggests a relationship between which of the following phenomena?

A) Protection of human rights abroad and military service

B) Spread of freedom abroad and defense of democracy at home

C) Defeat of tyrants abroad and establishment of democratic government at home

D) Investment in global democracies abroad and strengthening of patriotism at home

 GO ON TO THE NEXT PAGE

15. Which choice provides the best evidence for the answer to the previous question?

    A) Lines 23-28 ("These are . . . expectations")

    B) Lines 50-52 ("If the Congress . . . applause")

    C) Lines 71-76 ("That is no . . . of a bomb")

    D) Lines 92-95 ("Freedom means . . . unity of purpose")

16. In line 51, "pocketbooks" most nearly refers to

    A) local, state, and national taxes.

    B) war debt accumulated by the nation.

    C) citizens' individual monetary interests.

    D) Americans' personal investment in the defense industry.

17. In lines 71-73 ("That is no . . . generation"), President Roosevelt is most likely responding to what implicit counterclaim to his own argument?

    A) The spread of global democracy is idealistic and unrealistic.

    B) The defeat of tyrannical dictators in Europe is implausible.

    C) The commitment of the American people to the war effort is limited.

    D) The resources of the United States are insufficient to wage war abroad.

18. Which choice offers evidence that the spread of global democracy is achievable?

    A) Lines 46-47 ("No person . . . this program")

    B) Lines 54-55 ("we look forward . . . human freedoms")

    C) Lines 81-82 ("Since the beginning . . . in change")

    D) Line 95 ("Our strength . . . purpose")

19. In lines 60-64 ("The third is . . . world"), President Roosevelt sets a precedent by which he would most likely support which of the following policies?

    A) Military defense of political borders

    B) Investment in overseas business ventures

    C) Aid to nations struggling due to conflict and other causes

    D) Reduction of domestic services to spur job growth

20. The author refers to "the so-called new order of tyranny" primarily to

    A) connect the global conflict for human rights to citizens on a personal level.

    B) demonstrate the power of the global opposition to the United States.

    C) offer an alternative vision of the world without democracy.

    D) provide examples of the political and social revolutions underway.

GO ON TO THE NEXT PAGE

Questions 21-31 are based on the following passage and supplementary material.

The United States Constitution has been amended 27 times since its ratification. Rights such as freedom of speech, religion, and press, for example, are granted by the First Amendment. This passage focuses on the Nineteenth Amendment, which gave women the right to vote.

The American political landscape is constantly shifting on a myriad of issues, but the voting process itself has changed over the years as well. Electronic
Line ballot casting, for example, provides the public with
(5) instantaneous results, and statisticians are more accurate than ever at forecasting our next president. Voting has always been viewed as an intrinsic American right and was one of the major reasons for the nation's secession from Britain's monarchical
(10) rule. Unfortunately, although all men were constitutionally deemed "equal," true equality of the sexes was not extended to the voting booths until 1920.

The American women's suffrage movement began in 1848, when Elizabeth Cady Stanton and Lucretia
(15) Mott organized the Seneca Falls Convention. The meeting, initially an attempt to have an open dialogue about women's rights, drew a crowd of nearly three hundred women and included several dozen men. Topics ranged from a woman's role in society
(20) to law, but the issue of voting remained a contentious one. A freed slave named Frederick Douglass spoke eloquently about the importance of women in politics and swayed the opinion of those in attendance. At the end of the convention, one hundred
(25) people signed the Seneca Falls Declaration, which listed "immediate admission to all the rights and privileges which belong to [women] as citizens of the United States."

Stanton and Mott's first victory came thirty years
(30) later when a constitutional amendment allowing women to vote was proposed to Congress in 1878. Unfortunately, election practices were already a controversial issue, as unfair laws that diminished the African American vote had been passed during
(35) Reconstruction. Questionable literacy tests and a "vote tax" levied against the poor kept minority turnout to a minimum. And while several states

allowed women to vote, federal consensus was hardly as equitable. The rest of the world, however,
(40) was taking note—and women were ready to act.

In 1893, New Zealand allowed women the right to vote, although women could not run for office in New Zealand. Other countries began reviewing and ratifying their own laws as well. The United King-
(45) dom took small steps by allowing married women to vote in local elections in 1894. By 1902, all women in Australia could vote in elections, both local and parliamentary.

The suffrage movement in America slowly built
(50) momentum throughout the early twentieth century and exploded during World War I. President Woodrow Wilson called the fight abroad a war for democracy, which many suffragettes viewed as hypocritical. Democracy, after all, was hardly worth fighting for
(55) when half of a nation's population was disqualified based on gender. Public acts of civil disobedience, rallies, and marches galvanized pro-women advocates while undermining defenders of the status quo. Posters read "Kaiser Wilson" and called into ques-
(60) tion the authenticity of a free country with unjust laws. The cry for equality was impossible to ignore and, in 1919, with the support of President Wilson, Congress passed the Nineteenth Amendment to the Constitution. It was ratified one year later by two-
(65) thirds of the states, effectively changing the Constitution. Only one signatory from the original Seneca Falls Declaration lived long enough to cast her first ballot in a federal election.

America's election laws were far from equal
(70) for all, as tactics to dissuade or prohibit African Americans from effectively voting were still routinely employed. However, the suffrage movement laid the groundwork for future generations. Laws, like people's minds, could change over time. The
(75) civil rights movement in the mid- to late twentieth century brought an end to segregation and so-called Jim Crow laws that stifled African American advancement. The Voting Rights Act of 1965 was the final nail in the coffin; what emerged was a free
(80) nation guided by elections determined not by skin color or gender, but by the ballot box.

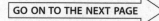
GO ON TO THE NEXT PAGE

Women's Suffrage in the United States

1848	Seneca Falls Convention.
1878	19th Amendment submitted; not ratified.
1911	Several states now grant women suffrage.
1914	Start of World War I.
1917	Picketing at the White House.
1918	Amendment passes in the House but fails in the Senate.
1919	Both the House and Senate pass the amendment.
1920	19th Amendment ratified.

21. The stance the author takes in the passage is best described as that of

A) an advocate of women's suffrage proposing a constitutional amendment.

B) a legislator reviewing the arguments for and against women's suffrage.

C) a scholar evaluating the evolution and impact of the women's suffrage movement.

D) a historian summarizing the motivations of women's suffrage leaders.

22. Lines 69-70 ("America's election laws . . . equal for all") most clearly support which explicit claim?

A) The founders of the Constitution did not provide for free and fair elections.

B) The United States still had work to do to secure equal voting rights for some people.

C) Most women in the United States did not want suffrage and equal rights.

D) The women's suffrage movement perpetuated discriminatory voting laws.

23. Which choice provides the best evidence for the answer to the previous question?

A) Lines 13-14 ("The American . . . in 1848")

B) Lines 41-42 ("In 1893 . . . to vote")

C) Lines 63-64 ("Congress . . . the Constitution")

D) Lines 78-79 ("The Voting Rights Act . . . the coffin")

24. As used in line 57, "galvanized" most nearly means

A) displaced.

B) divided.

C) excited.

D) organized.

25. The main rhetorical effect of lines 73-74 ("Laws, like . . . could change") is to

A) connect the success of legislative reform with shifts in public sentiment.

B) dissuade reformers from focusing on grassroots activity rather than political campaigns.

C) evaluate the effectiveness of judicial rulings based on popular response to public polls.

D) reject the need for legal actions and court proceedings to attain social change.

GO ON TO THE NEXT PAGE

26. As a whole, the passage most strongly suggests which conclusion?

    A) American government adapts to the changing needs and ideas of society.

    B) The best-organized reform movements are most likely to achieve their goals.

    C) The nation is more vulnerable to change during the confusion of wartime.

    D) The civil rights movement would not have happened without women suffragists.

27. Which choice provides the best evidence for the answer to the previous question?

    A) Lines 3-7 ("Electronic ballot casting . . . our next president")

    B) Lines 7-10 ("Voting has . . . monarchical rule")

    C) Lines 15-19 ("The meeting . . . dozen men")

    D) Lines 74-78 ("The civil rights . . . advancement")

28. The graphic most clearly illustrates which idea?

    A) The Nineteenth Amendment happened as a result of World War I.

    B) The states slowed reform of national voting rights laws.

    C) Women's suffrage resulted from a slow evolution of events.

    D) Acts of civil disobedience won support for suffrage in Congress.

29. In line 60, the word "authenticity" most nearly means

    A) reliability.

    B) realism.

    C) legitimacy.

    D) truth.

30. The passage suggests that President Wilson contributed to the success of the women's suffrage movement by

    A) circulating government propaganda in support of women's suffrage.

    B) framing the fight in World War I as a fight for democracy and freedom.

    C) engaging in a foreign war to distract the nation from political debate.

    D) working with legislators to write the Nineteenth Amendment.

31. The graphic helps support which statement referred to in the passage?

    A) Early women suffragists did not live to vote in national elections.

    B) The Nineteenth Amendment passed within a few years of its introduction.

    C) A majority of state representatives opposed women's suffrage in 1918.

    D) Many state governments approved suffrage before the federal government did.

Questions 32-42 are based on the following passages.

Passage 1

Coffee is a pillar of the world economy, generating both jobs and profits. The plant produced revenue to the tune of $15.4 billion in 2013 alone.
Line The coffee industry is also one of the world's largest
(5) employers, supporting 26 million employees. Because of the global importance of coffee, scientists at the University at Buffalo and their international colleagues were compelled to sequence the genome of the most popular coffee plant. In the genome lies
(10) the secrets of the bold flavor that people around the world have come to enjoy daily, as well as the caffeine kick that comes along with it. This new genetic information can be used to expand the market by creating new types of coffee varieties. The results of
(15) the study can also safeguard the existing industry. Scientists can now modify the genetic material of

the coffee plant. Heartier strains of popular coffee types can be created so that they are resistant to drought, disease, and bugs.

(20)   Researchers began their work by sequencing the genome of the type of coffee that makes up 30 percent of all coffee production. The conclusions drawn from this study will help save money and resources during the coffee production process.

(25) Researchers were able to isolate the genetic information of the enzymes in the coffee plant that produce caffeine. With this information, it may be possible to reduce or eliminate caffeine from coffee. This would remove a costly step in the current process

(30) of extracting caffeine from the coffee beans, while expanding the coffee market to people who avoid caffeine for health reasons, such as high blood pressure or pregnancy. The same research team plans to sequence the genome of other types of coffee in

(35) the future. It is their hope that the information will benefit the coffee producer, consumer, and also the environment.

Passage 2

The Gibbon Genome Sequencing Consortium has successfully sequenced the genome of the Northern

(40) white-cheeked gibbon. Both gibbons and humans have DNA that changes during the course of their lifetime. Some DNA changes in humans are the result of mutations, which cause cancer and other diseases. The changes in gibbons' DNA have resulted

(45) in many changes to the species over a very short period of time. Although gibbons are close relatives to humans, their DNA changes do not cause disease. Understanding the pattern of the gibbon genome might turn out to be very important to humans. If

(50) these changes in DNA can be understood, scientists may be able to use the information to better understand human disease.

Cancer and other genetic diseases are caused by faulty gene regulation. Scientists have sought to under-

(55) stand human biology through the lens of gibbon DNA structures for some time. Until now, there has simply been too much information to analyze. The endless rearrangements made it difficult to align gibbon DNA to that of humans, but it has finally been accomplished.

(60) Scientists discovered a piece of DNA that is unique to the gibbon species. Gibbons have a specific repeat

element, or a piece of DNA that copies itself multiple times throughout the genome. Repeat elements, in both gibbons and humans, are related to the

(65) maintenance of genetic structures. Scientists hope to be able to answer the question "Why can gibbon DNA rearrange itself without causing diseases—unlike humans' DNA?" If this complicated biological question can be solved, scientists may be able to work

(70) backward in order to help stop cancer, heart failure, and other human disease related to genetic repeats.

32. Which of the following best describes the central idea of Passage 1?

A) Advancements in genome sequencing will lead to healthier food options worldwide.

B) Genome sequencing of coffee can increase the profitability of coffee as a commodity.

C) Removing caffeine from coffee will allow more people to drink and enjoy coffee.

D) The coffee trade is an important sector of the global economy.

33. The author of Passage 2 would most likely agree that

A) instead of studying nonhuman animals, scientists should look for a way to stop human DNA from changing when it replicates itself.

B) sequencing the genome of other nonhuman primates could yield results that would be beneficial to people.

C) the benefits of genome sequencing of gibbons and other nonhuman animals does not justify the great expense and resources used.

D) scientists will be able to cure cancer once the mystery is solved of how the DNA of gibbons replicates itself without causing disease.

GO ON TO THE NEXT PAGE

34. Passage 1 most strongly suggests that

    A) the coffee industry will fail without new developments stemming from genome sequencing.

    B) newly developed varieties of coffee plants are more expensive for consumers than are existing varieties.

    C) future research will lead to developments that could increase the profitability for coffee producers.

    D) genome sequencing of coffee plants could help scientists understand diseases that affect humans.

35. Which choice provides the best evidence for the answer to the previous question?

    A) Lines 5-9 ("Because of the global . . . coffee plant")

    B) Lines 16-17 ("Scientists can . . . coffee plant")

    C) Lines 20-22 ("Researchers began . . . coffee production")

    D) Lines 28-33 ("This would remove . . . pregnancy")

36. Passage 2 most strongly suggests which of the following?

    A) The genetic makeup of the Northern white-cheeked gibbon is more similar to that of humans than to other primates.

    B) More research is needed before the findings of scientists studying the DNA of gibbons can be used to cure disease in humans.

    C) Many diseases and illnesses that affect humans can only be understood by studying the DNA of plants and other animals.

    D) Cancer and other diseases can be eliminated completely if enough funding is given to scientific research.

37. Which choice provides the best evidence for the answer to the previous question?

    A) Lines 40-44 ("Both gibbons . . . diseases")

    B) Lines 54-56 ("Scientists have sought . . . some time")

    C) Lines 63-65 ("Repeat elements . . . genetic structures")

    D) Lines 68-71 ("If this . . . genetic repeats")

38. Which of the following best summarizes a shared purpose of the two authors?

    A) To explain how genome sequencing in animals and plants can benefit people in unexpected ways

    B) To summarize how genome sequencing has changed the field of medicine and the study of diseases

    C) To inform readers about how scientific research can be applied to improving the world economy

    D) To convince readers to support funding for research in genome sequencing of plants and animals

39. As used in line 8, "compelled" most nearly means

    A) forced.

    B) driven.

    C) required.

    D) constrained.

40. As used in line 65, "maintenance" most nearly means

    A) preservation.

    B) protection.

    C) organization.

    D) repair.

GO ON TO THE NEXT PAGE ⟶

41. Which point is the author of Passage 1 trying to make by using the phrase "a pillar of the world economy" in line 1 to refer to the coffee industry?

    A) Research into the coffee plant is important and should be continued.

    B) The coffee industry plays a significant role in global economics.

    C) Many jobs will be lost if the coffee industry goes into decline.

    D) The coffee industry provides financial stability for millions of people worldwide.

42. Which of the following can reasonably be inferred based on the information in both passages?

    A) Studying the genomes of animals closely related to humans can help scientists learn about diseases that affect humans.

    B) Expanding the customer base of the coffee industry will lead to higher profits and increase the stability of the global economy.

    C) The scientists who study coffee and those who study gibbons could learn more by collaborating.

    D) The genomes of other plants and nonhuman animals hold secrets that can benefit people and are worthy of exploration.

Questions 43-52 are based on the following passage and supplementary material.

In 1948, Swiss chemist George de Mestral was impressed with the clinging power of burrs snagged in his dog's fur and on his pant legs after he returned
Line from a hike. While examining the burrs under a
(5) microscope, he observed many hundreds of small fibers that grabbed like hooks. He experimented with replicas of the burrs and eventually invented Velcro,® a synthetic clinging fabric that was first marketed as "the zipperless zipper." In the 1960s,

(10) NASA used de Mestral's invention on space suits, and now, of course, we see it everywhere.

You might say that de Mestral was the father of biomimicry, an increasingly essential field that studies nature, looking for efficiencies in materials and
(15) systems, and asks the question "How can our homes, our electronics, and our cities work better?" As one biomimetics company puts it: "Nature is the largest laboratory that ever existed and ever will."

Architecture is one field that is constantly
(20) exploring new ways to incorporate biomimicry. Architects have studied everything from beehives to beaver dams to learn how to best use materials, geometry, and physics in buildings. Termite mounds, for example, very efficiently regulate temperature,
(25) humidity, and airflow, so architects in Zimbabwe are working to apply what they've learned from termite mounds to human-made structures.

Says Michael Pawlyn, author of *Biomimicry in Architecture,* "If you look beyond the nice shapes
(30) in nature and understand the principles behind them, you can find some adaptations that can lead to new, innovative solutions that are radically more resource-efficient. It's the direction we need to take in the coming decades."

(35) Designers in various professional fields are drawing on biomimicry; for example, in optics, scientists have examined the surface of insect eyes in hopes of reducing glare on handheld device screens. Engineers in the field of robotics worked to replicate the
(40) property found in a gecko's feet that allows adhesion to smooth surfaces.

Sometimes what scientists learn from nature isn't more advanced, but simpler. The abalone shrimp, for example, makes its shell out of calcium carbonate,
(45) the same material as soft chalk. It's not a rare or complex substance, but the unique arrangement of the material in the abalone's shell makes it extremely tough. The walls of the shell contain microscopic pieces of calcium carbonate stacked like bricks,
(50) which are bound together using proteins just as concrete mortar is used. The result is a shell three thousand times harder than chalk and as tough as Kevlar® (the material used in bullet-proof vests).

GO ON TO THE NEXT PAGE ⇨

Often it is necessary to look at the nanoscale
(55) structures of a living material's exceptional properties
in order to re-create it synthetically. Andrew Parker,
an evolutionary biologist, looked at the skin of the
thorny devil (a type of lizard) under a scanning elec-
tron microscope, in search of the features that let the
(60) animal channel water from its back to its mouth.

Examples like this from the animal world abound.
Scientists have learned that colorful birds don't
always have pigment in their wings but are sometimes completely brown; it's the layers of keratin
(65) in their wings that produce color. Different colors,
which have varying wavelengths, reflect differently
through keratin. The discovery of this phenomenon
can be put to use in creating paints and cosmetics
that won't fade or chip. At the same time, paint for
(70) outdoor surfaces can be made tougher by copying
the structures found in antler bone. Hearing aids
are being designed to capture sound as well as the
ears of the *Ormia* fly do. And why can't we have a
self-healing material like our own skin? Researchers
(75) at the Beckman Institute at the University of Illinois
are creating just that; they call it an "autonomic
materials system." A raptor's feathers, a whale's fluke,
a mosquito's proboscis—all have functional features
we can learn from.

(80) The driving force behind these innovations, aside
from improved performance, is often improved
energy efficiency. In a world where nonrenewable energy resources are dwindling and carbon
emissions threaten the planet's health, efficiency has
(85) never been more important. Pawlyn agrees: "For
me, biomimicry is one of the best sources of inno-
vation to get to a world of zero waste because those
are the rules under which biological life has had to
exist."

(90) Biomimicry is a radical field and one whose prac-
titioners need to be radically optimistic, as Pawlyn
is when he says, "We could use natural products
such as cellulose, or even harvest carbon from the
atmosphere to create bio-rock."

Tiny florets in a sunflower's center are arranged in an
interlocking spiral, which inspired engineers in the
design of this solar power plant. Mirrors positioned
at the same angle as the florets bounce light toward
the power plant's central tower.

Adapted from David Ferris, "Innovate: Solar Designs
from Nature." © 2014 by Sierra Club.

43. The central idea of the passage is primarily concerned with

A) the field of biomimicry, the study of materials
and systems found in nature and replicated in
ways that benefit people.

B) the work of George de Mestral, the
Swiss chemist who invented Velcro® after
observing burrs under a microscope.

C) the ways in which architects use termite
mounds as models for human-made structures in Zimbabwe.

D) how scientists are seeking ways to improve
energy efficiency as nonrenewable energy
sources decline.

44. Which choice provides the best evidence for the
answer to the previous question?

A) Lines 1-6 ("In 1948 . . . hooks")

B) Lines 12-18 ("You might say . . . ever will'")

C) Lines 23-27 ("Termite mounds . . . structures")

D) Lines 80-85 ("The driving . . . more
important")

 GO ON TO THE NEXT PAGE ⟩

45. The author includes a quote in paragraph 4 in order to

    A) explain why architects are looking to biomimicry for solutions in architecture.

    B) provide an argument for more scientists to study biomimicry.

    C) give an explanation as to why someone might choose a career in architecture.

    D) provide a counterargument to the author's central claim.

46. Based on the information in paragraph 6, how does the shell of an abalone shrimp compare with soft chalk?

    A) The essential building blocks are arranged in a similar manner, but the material that makes up the shell of an abalone shrimp is harder.

    B) Both are made from the same essential building blocks, but the shell of the abalone shrimp is much harder because of the manner in which the materials are arranged.

    C) The essential building blocks of both are the same, but the abalone shrimp shell is harder because the soft chalk lacks a protein binding the materials together.

    D) They are made from different essential building blocks, but they have a similar hardness because the materials are arranged in a similar manner.

47. In paragraph 9, what is the most likely reason that the author included the quote from Pawlyn about efficiency?

    A) To convince readers that Pawlyn is an expert in his field

    B) To prove that great strides are being made in creating products that do not generate waste

    C) To demonstrate the limits of what biomimicry can achieve

    D) To support the statement that energy efficiency "has never been more important"

48. In line 30, "principles" most nearly means

    A) sources.

    B) attitudes.

    C) standards.

    D) theories.

49. It can be reasonably inferred from the passage that

    A) more scientists will utilize solutions developed through biomimicry in the future.

    B) the field of biomimicry will eventually decline as more nonrenewable resources are discovered.

    C) scientists will leave the fields they are currently working in and begin research in biomimicry.

    D) doctors will create a self-healing skin called an "autonomic materials system" using methods based in biomimicry.

GO ON TO THE NEXT PAGE

50. Which choice provides the best evidence for the answer to the previous question?

    A) Lines 35-38 ("Designers . . . screens")

    B) Lines 54-56 ("Often it is . . . synthetically")

    C) Lines 61-79 ("Examples like . . . learn from")

    D) Lines 89-94 ("Biomimicry . . . bio-rock")

51. As used in line 90, "radical" most nearly means

    A) pervasive.

    B) drastic.

    C) essential.

    D) revolutionary.

52. The graphic and caption that accompany this passage help illustrate how biomimicry can be used to

    A) make a solar plant more attractive.

    B) decrease waste generated by energy sources.

    C) improve the efficiency of existing models.

    D) replicate a pattern common in nature.

IF YOU FINISH BEFORE TIME IS CALLED, YOU MAY CHECK YOUR WORK ON THIS SECTION ONLY. DO NOT TURN TO ANY OTHER SECTION IN THE TEST. **STOP**

WRITING AND LANGUAGE TEST

35 Minutes—44 Questions

Turn to Section 2 of your answer sheet to answer the questions in this section.

Directions: Each passage below is accompanied by a number of questions. For some questions, you will consider how the passage might be revised to improve the expression of ideas. For other questions, you will consider how the passage might be edited to correct errors in sentence structure, usage, or punctuation. A passage or a question may be accompanied by one or more graphics (such as a table or graph) that you will consider as you make revising and editing decisions.

Some questions will direct you to an underlined portion of a passage. Other questions will direct you to a location in a passage or ask you to think about the passage as a whole.

After reading each passage, choose the answer to each question that most effectively improves the quality of writing in the passage or that makes the passage conform to the conventions of standard written English. Many questions include a "NO CHANGE" option. Choose that option if you think the best choice is to leave the relevant portion of the passage as it is.

Questions 1-11 are based on the following passage.

The Age of the Librarian

When Kristen Harris ❶ is in college, she worked in her university's library and was constantly told, "You really should be studying to be a librarian; this is ❷ your home" however Harris was pursuing a bachelor's degree in elementary education at the time. Little did she realize that becoming a school librarian was indeed ❸ elective. During the 21st century, the age of information, what could be more necessary than an individual trained to gather, process, and disseminate information? So, after teaching children in the classroom, Harris went back to school to earn her Master of Library Science degree.

1. A) NO CHANGE
   B) has been
   C) was
   D) had been

2. A) NO CHANGE
   B) your home," however Harris
   C) your home."; However Harris
   D) your home." However, Harris

3. A) NO CHANGE
   B) imminent
   C) threatening
   D) optional

GO ON TO THE NEXT PAGE >

Today, Harris is preparing a story time for a group of young students. As it has done with everything else, the technology revolution has elevated the school library to "Library 2.0," and Harris's tablet-integrated story time begins when she projects images for *The Very Cranky Bear* onto a projector screen. As a child, Harris got excited whenever a puppet appeared during story time, but now she uses an interactive app (application software) to enhance her own story time and ❹ <u>integrate</u> this next generation of children.

As she introduces the children to the problem of cheering up a cranky ❺ <u>bear, Harris sees Miguel</u> scouring the library shelves for another book by a popular author. ❻ <u>Miguel had said asking Harris for a book two weeks earlier "If you have any funny stories, I like those."</u>

4. A) NO CHANGE
    B) enervate
    C) energize
    D) elucidate

5. A) NO CHANGE
    B) bear; Harris sees Miguel
    C) bear: Harris sees Miguel
    D) bear Harris sees Miguel

6. A) NO CHANGE
    B) Miguel had said, "If you have any funny stories, I like those, "asking Harris for a book two weeks earlier.
    C) Asking Harris for a book two weeks earlier, Miguel had said, "If you have any funny stories, I like those."
    D) Miguel asked Harris for a book two weeks earlier had said, "If you have any funny stories, I like those."

GO ON TO THE NEXT PAGE ⟶

"It will always be satisfying," reflects Harris, "the act of finding books for students and having them return to say, 'I really liked that one. Are there any more by that author?'"

[7] These days, Harris would call herself a media mentor as much as a librarian because she regularly visits her favorite websites for reviews of apps and other digital tools to suggest to students and parents. Librarians have always been an important resource for families in a community, but this importance has grown exponentially because of the advent of technology. Librarians are offering guidance about new media to address the changing information needs in our communities. Furthermore, libraries are becoming increasingly technology driven, for example,

7. Which sentence could be added to the paragraph to most effectively establish its main idea?

A) Harris maintains active profiles on multiple social media networks to better connect with her students.

B) The role of the school librarian has changed rapidly to meet the needs of students who are digital citizens.

C) Librarians still perform many traditional tasks such as putting great literature in the hands of their students.

D) In the future, many school libraries are unlikely to have books on the shelves because students prefer electronic media.

GO ON TO THE NEXT PAGE

8 enabling access to collections of other libraries, offering remote access to databases, or they house video production studios. So, in Harris's opinion, librarians must be masters of the digital world. **9**

Harris finishes her story time and heads across the library. A young student stops her and asks, "Ms. Harris, what's new in the library?"

8. A) NO CHANGE
   B) by enabling access to collections of other libraries, offering remote access to databases, or by housing video production studios.
   C) they enable access to collections of other libraries, offering remote access to databases, or they house video production studios.
   D) enabling access to collections of other libraries, offering remote access to databases, or housing video production studios.

9. Which sentence would provide evidence to effectively support the main idea of the paragraph?
   A) Harris sponsors a weekly "Fun Read" book discussion club that is well attended by many of the students at her school.
   B) Librarians continue to help students and teachers locate the perfect book in the library's collection.
   C) Teachers frequently ask Harris to recommend educational apps to support early literacy for their students.
   D) Many parents are concerned with online safety and digital citizenship due to the proliferation of social media.

GO ON TO THE NEXT PAGE ⟶

⑩ <u>She chuckles</u> and thinks about the many collections, services, and programs their school library offers. "Have you seen the Trendy 10 list? You read the books on the list and blog **⑪** <u>your</u> ideas about them. I'll set you up with a password and username so you can blog," says Harris. In this library full of information, she's the gatekeeper.

Questions 12-22 are based on the following passage.

Unforeseen Consequences: The Dark Side of the Industrial Revolution

There is no doubt that the Industrial Revolution guided America through the nascent stages of independence **⑫** <u>and into being a robust economic powerhouse.</u> Inventions like the cotton gin revolutionized the textile industry, and the steam engine ushered in the advent of expeditious cross-country distribution.

The Industrial Revolution marked a shift from an agrarian to an industry-centered society. People eschewed farming in favor of **⑬** <u>more lucrative enterprises in urban areas which put a strain on</u> existing local resources. Necessary goods such as **⑭** <u>food crops, vegetables, and meat products</u> also had to be shipped in order to meet the dietary needs of a consolidated population. And because there were fewer people farming, food had to travel farther and in higher quantities to meet demand. Issues like carbon dioxide emissions, therefore, arose not only as byproducts of industrial production but also from the delivery of these products. As a result, booming metropolises needed additional lumber, metal, and coal shipped from rural areas to sustain population and industrial growth.

10. A) NO CHANGE
    B) He chuckles
    C) Harris chuckles
    D) They chuckle

11. A) NO CHANGE
    B) they're
    C) you're
    D) their

12. A) NO CHANGE
    B) and into the role of a robust economic powerhouse.
    C) and turned into a robust economic powerhouse.
    D) and then became a robust economic powerhouse.

13. A) NO CHANGE
    B) more lucrative enterprises in urban areas, which put a strain on
    C) more lucrative enterprises in urban areas; which put a strain on
    D) more lucrative enterprises in urban areas. Which put a strain on

14. A) NO CHANGE
    B) food
    C) food crops
    D) vegetables and meat products

GO ON TO THE NEXT PAGE →

15 [1] The negative effects of such expansion on humans were immediately apparent. Improper water sanitization led to cholera outbreaks in big cities. [2] Miners suffered from black lung after spending hours harvesting coal in dark caverns. [3] Combusted fossil fuels ⓰ <u>released unprecedented amounts of human-made carbon dioxide into the air</u>, resulting in respiratory ailments. [4] The fact remains that smog, now an internationally recognized buzzword, simply did not exist before the factories that produced it.

The critical impact on the environment must also ⓱ <u>be taken into account. Proper regulations</u> were either not in place or not enforced.

15. To effectively transition from paragraph 2, which sentence should begin paragraph 3?

A) Sentence 1

B) Sentence 2

C) Sentence 3

D) Sentence 4

16. Which graphic would best support the underlined claim?

A) A line graph plotting an increase in atmospheric carbon dioxide over time

B) A pie chart comparing the present percentages of carbon dioxide and other atmospheric gases

C) A timeline tracking carbon dioxide emissions testing dates

D) A bar graph showing levels of atmospheric carbon dioxide in different locations

17. Which choice most effectively combines the sentences at the underlined portion?

A) be taken into account, and proper regulations

B) be taken into account since without proper regulations

C) be taken into account, as proper regulations

D) be taken into account; however, proper regulations

GO ON TO THE NEXT PAGE ⇨

Industrial waste was often disposed of in the nearest river or buried in landfills, where it ⑱ <u>polluted</u> groundwater essential for wildlife to thrive. Deforestation across the United States served the dual purpose of providing inhabitable land and wood, but it also caused animals to migrate or die out completely.

Although the Industrial Revolution heralded an age of consumer ease and excess, it also invited a cyclical process of destruction and reduced resources. ⑲ <u>Greenhouse gases were released into the atmosphere.</u> Numerous health problems caused by ⑳ <u>depressing</u> working conditions prevented rural emigrants from thriving. And the environment that had cradled humankind since its inception was slowly being ㉑ <u>degraded. All</u> in the name of progress. ㉒

18. A) NO CHANGE
    B) disturbed
    C) drained
    D) enhanced

19. Which choice should be added to the end of the underlined sentence to better support the claim in the preceding sentence?

    A) NO CHANGE
    B) while carbon dioxide-consuming trees were cut down to make way for new living spaces.
    C) and caused an increase in global temperatures as well as a rise in coastal sea levels.
    D) faster than they could be absorbed by the atmosphere's shrinking ozone layer.

20. A) NO CHANGE
    B) urban
    C) substandard
    D) developing

21. A) NO CHANGE
    B) degraded; all
    C) degraded! All
    D) degraded—all

GO ON TO THE NEXT PAGE

22. Which choice most effectively states the central idea of the essay on the previous page?

   A) The Industrial Revolution created a new consumer society that replaced the existing farming society.

   B) Politicians and historians today disagree about the true consequences of the Industrial Revolution.

   C) Although some analysts suggest that industrialization had many problems, its immense benefits outweigh these concerns.

   D) Unfortunately, progress came at the expense of environmental and ecological preservation and may well have ruined the future that once looked so bright.

Questions 23-33 are based on the following passage.

Remembering Freud

Psychology has grown momentously over the past century, largely due to the influence of Sigmund Freud, a pioneer of the field. This Austrian-born neurologist founded the practice of psychoanalysis and **23** began scientific study of the unconscious mind. **24** Since his career which ended in the mid-twentieth century, Freud has remained a common cultural and scientific reference point.

23. A) NO CHANGE
    B) continued
    C) spearheaded
    D) led to

24. A) NO CHANGE
    B) Since his career, which ended in the mid-twentieth century, Freud has remained
    C) Since his career ending in the mid-twentieth century; Freud has remained
    D) Since his career (ending in the mid-twentieth century) Freud has remained

GO ON TO THE NEXT PAGE

25 Even the abiding popularity of terms such as "id," "ego," or talking about a "Freudian slip" serves to indicate how this psychologist lingers powerfully in Western memory.

As neuroscience has progressed, many early practices and theories, including some of Freud's, have been dismissed as outdated, unscientific, or even harmful. Much of Freud's theory, clinical practice, and even lifestyle are now discredited. But when considered in his historical context, alongside the astounding progress catalyzed by his work, Freud's contribution was significant indeed.

26 Because he is now widely referred to as the Father of Psychoanalysis, Freud was among the first to develop the now-commonplace psychological method of inviting patients to freely speak. For Freud, this was both study and treatment. It helped doctors to understand patients, but more importantly it helped patients to understand themselves. Freud employed the classic (now largely outdated) psychiatric style in which the patient lies face-up on a clinical bed, allegedly enabling access to deep **27** parts of the mind. These recesses, better known as the unconscious or subconscious, fascinated Freud.

25. A) NO CHANGE
    B) Even the abiding popularity of terms such as the "id," "ego," or a "Freudian slip"
    C) Even the abiding popularity of terms such as talking about an "id," "ego," or "Freudian slip"
    D) Even the abiding popularity of terms such as "id," "ego," or "Freudian slip"

26. A) NO CHANGE
    B) Widely remembered as the Father of Psychoanalysis, Freud was among the first to develop the now-commonplace psychological method of inviting patients to freely speak.
    C) Freud was among the first to develop the now-commonplace psychological method of inviting patients to freely speak, which is why he is now widely remembered as the Father of Psychoanalysis.
    D) Although he is widely remembered as the Father of Psychoanalysis, Freud was among the first to develop the now-commonplace psychological method of inviting patients to freely speak.

27. A) NO CHANGE
    B) recesses
    C) places
    D) components

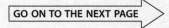 GO ON TO THE NEXT PAGE

28 He believed that uncovering repressed memories, was necessary for recovery. For Freud, understanding the activity of the innermost mind was essential. **29** In dealing with the conditions of patients, like neurosis or other psychological trauma, he suspected that there was a great deal going on beneath the "surface" of the psyche. He thought it was possible to reunite external, or conscious, thought with the internal,

28. A) NO CHANGE

    B) He believed that uncovering repressed memories, being necessary for recovery.

    C) He believed that uncovering repressed memories was necessary for recovery.

    D) He believed that uncovering, repressed memories was necessary for recovery.

29. A) NO CHANGE

    B) In dealing with patients' conditions, like neurosis or other psychological trauma, he suspected that

    C) In dealing with patients like neurosis or other psychological trauma conditions he suspected that

    D) He suspected that, in dealing with patients' conditions like neurosis or other psychological trauma,

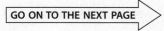GO ON TO THE NEXT PAGE

or unconscious. `30` Moreover, the method of inviting patients to speak and process their thoughts aloud remains central to today's psychological practice.

Freud altered the course of twentieth-century medicine by initiating what would become a grand, global conversation about the `31` <u>still vastly mysterious human mind before Freud, medicine</u> had barely scratched the surface in understanding mental health. Patients were met with very few answers, let alone recovery protocols. `32` <u>Through trial and error—scientific method in action—Freud's finding of a method that seemed to work.</u>

30. Which detail would provide the best support for the ideas presented in this section?

    A) At the same time that Freud practiced, many people were interested in spiritualism.

    B) Freud lived and worked mostly in London although he had originally trained in Austria.

    C) While some of Freud's more unusual practices have been criticized or abandoned, his interest in the unconscious altered the trajectory of the field.

    D) Psychologists today employ many theories, not just those developed by Freud.

31. A) NO CHANGE

    B) still vastly mysterious human mind. Before Freud, medicine

    C) still vastly mysterious human mind, before Freud, medicine

    D) still vastly mysterious human mind before Freud. Medicine

32. A) NO CHANGE

    B) Through trial and error—scientific method in action—Freud's finding a method that seems to work.

    C) Through trial and error—scientific method in action—Freud finds a method that seemed to work.

    D) Through trial and error—scientific method in action—Freud found a method that seemed to work.

GO ON TO THE NEXT PAGE ⟶

Since then, decades of ever-sharpening science have used his work as a launching pad. Therefore, as long as occasions arise to celebrate the progress of the field, Sigmund Freud will be remembered for groundbreaking work that enabled countless advances.

Questions 34-44 are based on the following passage and supplementary material.

Success in Montreal

The Montreal Protocol on Substances That Deplete the Ozone Layer is an international treaty that was created to ensure that steps would be taken to reverse damage to Earth's ozone layer and **34** preventing future damage. **35** It was signed in 1987. This document created restrictions on chemicals that were known to be dangerous to the protective barrier that the ozone layer offers Earth. Without the ozone layer, the sun's dangerous UV rays would alter our climate so drastically, life on land and in water would cease to exist.

33. A) NO CHANGE
    B) the field; Sigmund Freud will be remembered for ground-breaking work that
    C) the field Sigmund Freud will be remembered for ground-breaking work that
    D) the field Sigmund Freud will be remembered for ground-breaking work, and that

34. A) NO CHANGE
    B) to prevent
    C) prevented
    D) was preventing

35. Which choice most effectively combines the sentences in the underlined portion?
    A) Signed in 1987, this document
    B) Because it was signed in 1987, this document
    C) It was signed in 1987, and this document
    D) It was signed in 1987 so this document

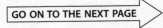
GO ON TO THE NEXT PAGE

A hole in Earth's ozone layer was discovered over Antarctica **36** <u>as long as two years prior</u> to the signing of the treaty. The discovery brought the human impact on the environment to the forefront of **37** <u>international conversation, the massive hole</u> was evidence that a global response was necessary and that large-scale action was needed. The Montreal Protocol became effective January 1, 1989, and nearly 100 gases deemed dangerous to the ozone layer have been phased out. As a result, **38** <u>the size of the ozone hole decreased significantly during the 1990s.</u>

Now that a substantial amount of time has passed since the treaty was put into place, the effects can begin to be **39** <u>looked at</u>. As a part of the treaty, the Montreal Protocol's Scientific Assessment Panel was created to gauge **40** <u>their</u> effect on the hole in the ozone layer.

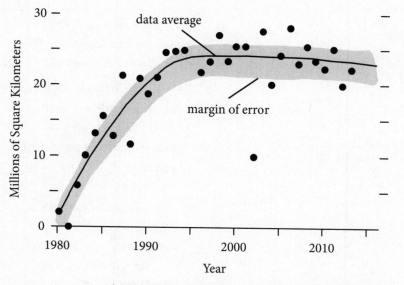

Size of Ozone Hole

Adapted from Ozone Hole Watch, NASA Goddard Space Flight Center.

36. A) NO CHANGE
    B) long ago, two years prior
    C) two years prior
    D) years prior

37. A) NO CHANGE
    B) international conversation, yet the massive hole
    C) international conversation. The massive hole
    D) international conversation, so the massive hole

38. Which choice completes the sentence with accurate data based on the graphic?
    A) NO CHANGE
    B) the average size of the ozone hole leveled off beginning in the 1990s.
    C) the average size of the ozone hole decreased beginning in the 2000s.
    D) the average size of the ozone hole increased beginning in the 1980s.

39. A) NO CHANGE
    B) controlled
    C) measured
    D) governed

40. A) NO CHANGE
    B) its
    C) it's
    D) there

GO ON TO THE NEXT PAGE

The Panel has since reported the results every four years. The Panel predicts that the ozone layer will return to its former state of health by 2060–2075. [41]

   While the treaty is already an obvious success, work continues to ensure that human strides in technology and industry do not reverse the healing process. The Montreal Protocol's Multilateral Fund was established to help developing countries transition away from the consumption and production of harmful chemicals. So far, over $3 billion has been invested by the Fund. The developing countries are referred to as "Article 5 countries." [42]

41. Which choice could be added to paragraph 3 to most effectively convey its central idea?

A) It is the Panel's current estimation that the ozone layer is beginning to heal, but the rate of progress is slow.

B) The Panel meets once a year to assess the increase or decrease of each gas that has been identified as dangerous.

C) Of much concern to the Panel was the effect of ultraviolet radiation on the ozone layer.

D) The Panel has recently updated procedures for the nomination and selection of its membership.

42. Which sentence in paragraph 4 provides the least support for the central idea of the paragraph?

A) While the treaty is already an obvious success, work continues to ensure that human strides in technology and industry do not reverse the healing process.

B) The Montreal Protocol's Multilateral Fund was established to help developing countries transition away from the consumption and production of harmful chemicals.

C) So far, over $3 billion has been invested by the Fund.

D) The developing countries are referred to as "Article 5 countries."

GO ON TO THE NEXT PAGE

[1] The Montreal Protocol is a living document. [2] A current amendment proposition has been put forth by the United States, Mexico, and Canada jointly. [3] It aims to cut down on harmful gases that were put into use as an alternative to the gases specified in the original Montreal Protocol treaty. [4] It has been amended four times since its inception. [5] Combating the erosion of our ozone layer will take time and flexibility, but the research is clear: If humans stay conscious of what we emit into the atmosphere, we can not only stall the damage we have done in the past, but we can **43** change it. **44**

43. A) NO CHANGE
    B) switch
    C) invert
    D) reverse

44. For the sake of cohesion of this paragraph, sentence 4 should be placed

    A) where it is now.
    B) before sentence 1.
    C) after sentence 1.
    D) before sentence 3.

ESSAY TEST

50 Minutes

The essay gives you an opportunity to show how effectively you can read and comprehend a passage and write an essay analyzing the passage. In your essay, you should demonstrate that you have read the passage carefully, present a clear and logical analysis, and use language precisely.

Your essay must be written on the lines provided in your answer booklet; except for the planning page of the answer booklet, you will receive no other paper on which to write. You will have enough space if you write on every line, avoid wide margins, and keep your handwriting to a reasonable size. Remember that people who are not familiar with your handwriting will read what you write. Try to write or print so that what you are writing is legible to those readers.

You have 50 minutes to read the passage and write an essay in response to the prompt provided inside this booklet.

1. Do not write your essay in this booklet. Only what you write on the lined pages of your answer booklet will be evaluated.

2. An off-topic essay will not be evaluated.

As you read the passage below, consider how Morris uses

- evidence, such as facts or examples, to support claims.

- reasoning to develop ideas and to connect claims and evidence.

- stylistic or persuasive elements, such as word choice or appeals to emotion, to add power to the ideas expressed.

Adapted from Elisabeth Woodbridge Morris's essay "The Tyranny of Things." In this portion, Morris paints a portrait of American consumerism in 1917 and offers a distinct perspective on the joy of freedom from "things, things, things."

Two fifteen-year-old girls stood eyeing one another on first acquaintance. Finally one little girl said, "Which do you like best, people or things?" The other little girl said, "Things." They were friends at once.

I suppose we all go through a phase when we like things best; and not only like them, but want to possess them under our hand. The passion for accumulation is upon us. We make "collections," we fill our rooms, our walls, our tables, our desks, with things, things, things.

Many people never pass out of this phase. They never see a flower without wanting to pick it and put it in a vase, they never enjoy a book without wanting to own it, nor a picture without wanting to hang it on their walls. They keep photographs of all their friends and Kodak albums of all the places they visit, they save all their theater programmes and dinner cards, they bring home all their alpenstocks.* Their houses are filled with an undigested mass of things, like the terminal moraine where a glacier dumps at length everything it has picked up during its progress through the lands.

But to some of us a day comes when we begin to grow weary of things. We realize that we do not possess them; they possess us. Our books are a burden to us, our pictures have destroyed every restful wall-space,

---

* alpenstocks: strong pointed poles used by mountain climbers

GO ON TO THE NEXT PAGE

our china is a care, our photographs drive us mad, our programmes and alpenstocks fill us with loathing. We feel stifled with the sense of things, and our problem becomes, not how much we can accumulate, but how much we can do without. We send our books to the village library, and our pictures to the college settlement. Such things as we cannot give away, and have not the courage to destroy, we stack in the garret, where they lie huddled in dim and dusty heaps, removed from our sight, to be sure, yet still faintly importunate.

Then, as we breathe more freely in the clear space that we have made for ourselves, we grow aware that we must not relax our vigilance, or we shall be once more overwhelmed. . . .

It extends to all our doings. For every event there is a "souvenir." We cannot go to luncheon and meet our friends but we must receive a token to carry away. Even our children cannot have a birthday party, and play games, and eat good things, and be happy. The host must receive gifts from every little guest, and provide in return some little remembrance for each to take home. Truly, on all sides we are beset, and we go lumbering along through life like a ship encrusted with barnacles, which can never cut the waves clean and sure and swift until she has been scraped bare again. And there seems little hope for us this side our last port.

And to think that there was a time when folk had not even that hope! When a man's possessions were burned with him, so that he might, forsooth, have them all about him in the next world! Suffocating thought! To think one could not even then be clear of things, and make at least a fresh start! That must, indeed, have been in the childhood of the race.

Once upon a time, when I was very tired, I chanced to go away to a little house by the sea. . . . There was nothing in the house to demand care, to claim attention, to cumber my consciousness with its insistent, unchanging companionship. There was nothing but a shelter, and outside, the fields and marshes, the shore and the sea. These did not have to be taken down and put up and arranged and dusted and cared for. They were not things at all, they were powers, presences. . . .

If we could but free ourselves once for all, how simple life might become! One of my friends, who, with six young children and only one servant, keeps a spotless house and a soul serene, told me once how she did it. "My dear, once a month I give away every single thing in the house that we do not imperatively need. It sounds wasteful, but I don't believe it really is. . . ."

Write an essay in which you explain how Morris builds an argument to persuade her audience that possessions are oppressive. In your essay, analyze how Morris uses one or more of the features listed in the box that precedes the passage (or features of your own choice) to strengthen the logic and persuasiveness of her argument. Be sure that your analysis focuses on the most relevant features of the passage.

Your essay should not explain whether you agree with Morris's claims, but rather explain how Morris builds an argument to persuade her audience.

ANSWER KEY
READING TEST

1. A	14. B	27. D	40. A
2. B	15. D	28. C	41. B
3. C	16. C	29. C	42. D
4. C	17. A	30. B	43. A
5. A	18. D	31. D	44. B
6. C	19. C	32. B	45. A
7. D	20. C	33. B	46. B
8. A	21. C	34. C	47. D
9. D	22. B	35. D	48. D
10. A	23. D	36. B	49. A
11. A	24. C	37. D	50. C
12. D	25. A	38. A	51. D
13. D	26. A	39. B	52. C

WRITING AND LANGUAGE TEST

1. C	12. B	23. C	34. B
2. D	13. B	24. B	35. A
3. B	14. B	25. D	36. C
4. C	15. A	26. B	37. C
5. A	16. A	27. B	38. B
6. C	17. C	28. C	39. C
7. B	18. A	29. B	40. B
8. D	19. B	30. C	41. A
9. C	20. C	31. B	42. D
10. C	21. D	32. D	43. D
11. A	22. D	33. A	44. C

ANSWERS & EXPLANATIONS

READING TEST

Anna Karenina

1. A
Difficulty: Easy

Category: Reading / Detail

Strategic Advice: Make sure to read the passage closely so events are clearly understood.

Getting to the Answer: The first paragraph explicitly states how Levin knew that Kitty was there. Choice (A) matches the information stated in the passage.

2. B
Difficulty: Medium

Category: Reading / Vocab-in-Context

Strategic Advice: Use context clues to help you distinguish the shades of meaning each word has.

Getting to the Answer: Two of the answer choices have a somewhat negative connotation. The author is not describing the scene in a negative way. In this passage, the word "swarmed" means "gathered." Therefore, (B) is the correct answer. The other words' connotations do not fit with the context of the sentence.

3. C
Difficulty: Hard

Category: Reading / Inference

Strategic Advice: Look for clues in the text that suggest what Levin is like.

Getting to the Answer: Emotionally charged phrases, such as "the rapture and the terror that seized on his heart," help reveal Levin's personality.

Choice (C) reflects the depiction of Levin as a passionate person.

4. C
Difficulty: Hard

Category: Reading / Command of Evidence

Strategic Advice: Eliminate answer choices that don't include a description of Levin.

Getting to the Answer: Because the excerpt focuses on Levin's feelings toward Kitty, evidence of the kind of person he is will probably reflect this. Choice (C) provides the best evidence.

5. A
Difficulty: Medium

Category: Reading / Global

Strategic Advice: The central theme of a passage is the insight about life that the author is trying to get across to the reader. Eliminate any themes that are not revealed by the experiences of Levin.

Getting to the Answer: Though you may personally agree with more than one of the themes presented, (A) is the only answer choice that is supported by details in the passage. Levin's feelings and actions support this theme.

6. C
Difficulty: Medium

Category: Reading / Inference

Strategic Advice: Examine the passage to see what other characters do in response to Levin.

Getting to the Answer: The other skaters go about their business. Most take little notice of Levin. Therefore, (C) is the correct answer.

7. D

Difficulty: Medium

Category: Reading / Command of Evidence

Strategic Advice: Reread each quote in the context of the passage. This will help you decide the correct answer.

Getting to the Answer: Of all the answer choices, Nikolay's way of greeting Levin is the strongest evidence that people think Levin seems normal. Choice (D) is the correct answer.

8. A

Difficulty: Medium

Category: Reading / Vocab-in-Context

Strategic Advice: The context of the passage can help reveal the meaning of the word. Insert each choice in the sentence to see which one makes the most sense.

Getting to the Answer: Levin speaks directly to his heart, asking it to behave. Choice (A), "begged," comes closest to meaning the same thing as "conjured" in this context.

9. D

Difficulty: Medium

Category: Reading / Rhetoric

Strategic Advice: Think about the entire scene described in the passage and decide why the author chose to describe Levin's heart as "throbbing."

Getting to the Answer: Choice (D) is the correct answer. The author chose this word to capture Levin's agitated state.

10. A

Difficulty: Hard

Category: Reading / Rhetoric

Strategic Advice: Eliminate answer choices that are clearly not representative of the author's feelings or attitude about Levin.

Getting to the Answer: The author presents Levin's situation as one that is painful. The passage's tone suggests that Levin is worthy of the reader's empathy. Choice (A) fits this tone.

Franklin Delano Roosevelt Speech

11. A

Difficulty: Hard

Category: Reading / Rhetoric

Strategic Advice: Watch out for choices that indicate broad supporting goals. The correct answer will reflect the specific intent of President Roosevelt in giving this address.

Getting to the Answer: The introduction to the passage states that President Roosevelt reveals his intention to preserve and spread American democratic ideals. Roosevelt's remarks regarding taxation, patriotism, and sacrifice suggest that he wishes to gain the support of the American people for these goals and to persuade them to connect the fight for global democracy with their own democratic interests. Choice (A) makes clear the president's purpose in winning citizens' support for the battles abroad.

12. D

Difficulty: Hard

Category: Reading / Command of Evidence

Strategic Advice: Be careful of choices that do not provide direct evidence to support the president's purpose. The correct answer will relate specifically to the stated purpose, or intent, of the passage.

Getting to the Answer: President Roosevelt makes clear that his intention is to provide support for global efforts to end tyranny and spread democracy and to garner the support of the American people for these goals. In the previous question, his stated purpose is "to make its people conscious of their individual stake in the preservation of democratic life in America." The two elements of that purpose are the American people and the preservation of democratic life. Only (D) provides direct evidence for the previous question.

13. D

Difficulty: Easy

Category: Reading / Vocab-in-Context

Strategic Advice: All answer choices are alternate meanings of the word "sacrifice." The correct answer will relate directly to the context of the passage.

Getting to the Answer: Despite the fact that Roosevelt gave the speech on the eve of America's involvement in World War II, neither B nor C is the meaning he's after. Choice (D), "surrender of interests to a greater good," is the correct answer.

14. B

Difficulty: Hard

Category: Reading / Inference

Strategic Advice: Keep in mind that you're looking for a relationship that is suggested, not stated. To reach the correct answer, you must infer, or make a logical guess, based on information in the passage.

Getting to the Answer: The correct answer will provide support for the stated purpose of the passage while demonstrating a logical relationship. Choice (B) provides support for the stated goal of winning support among U.S. citizens for the spread of democracy abroad. It does so by suggesting that the security of U.S. democracy depends on the advancement of human rights and freedoms globally.

15. D

Difficulty: Medium

Category: Reading / Command of Evidence

Strategic Advice: Avoid answers that provide evidence for incorrect answers to the previous question. The correct answer will use language reflective of the correct answer above to demonstrate a relationship.

Getting to the Answer: Principles and ideas such as democracy, freedom, and protection of human rights are used interchangeably throughout Roosevelt's speech. The lines in (D) draw the connection between freedom at home and freedom everywhere.

16. C

Difficulty: Easy

Category: Reading / Vocab-in-Context

Strategic Advice: Substitute each answer choice for the word in question and decide which one fits the context provided in the passage.

Getting to the Answer: In the context of the passage, (C) works best. It draws a distinction between individual citizens' monetary interests, or their pocketbooks, and the cause of patriotism, or the greater good.

17. A

Difficulty: Medium

Category: Reading / Rhetoric

Strategic Advice: Keep in mind that the correct answer will relate directly to the meaning of the elements in the identified lines.

Getting to the Answer: President Roosevelt is arguing against those who would oppose the overarching goal of his speech, namely to recruit American public support for the war effort and the spread of democracy overseas. Choice (A) fits best; Roosevelt asserts that his goals are realistic and attainable, not just idealistic visions, as his opponents might claim.

18. D

Difficulty: Medium

Category: Reading / Rhetoric

Strategic Advice: Be wary of answers like A and B that seem to offer specific advice or state specific goals relevant to the purpose of the passage without suggesting how those goals might be achieved. The correct answer will offer a tool, a condition, or another asset for achieving the passage's claim—in this case, the spread of democracy.

Getting to the Answer: The previous question identifies that President Roosevelt considers the spread of global democracy achievable. This question asks you to identify how the president envisions achieving that purpose. Choice (D) matches the intent. In this line, President Roosevelt identifies "our unity of purpose" as an asset that will help achieve his goal.

19. C
Difficulty: Hard

Category: Reading / Inference

Strategic Advice: Be careful of answers that cite other policies that the president might support that are not related to the lines quoted. The correct answer will relate directly to the specific lines in question.

Getting to the Answer: In this speech, Roosevelt identifies four freedoms that he views the United States as obligated to defend. The freedom from want signifies a commitment to helping struggling populations at home and abroad. Choice (C) fits. The president urges economic understandings among nations to help those in need.

20. C
Difficulty: Medium

Category: Reading / Rhetoric

Strategic Advice: Be careful of answers like A that offer other viable uses of rhetoric within the larger passage. The correct answer will relate specifically to the text cited in the question.

Getting to the Answer: Roosevelt suggests that the preservation of American freedoms cannot exist without the preservation of human rights on a global scale. To cement this connection, he contrasts democratic movements with tyrannical movements occurring in the world. Choice (C) is the correct answer. President Roosevelt references "the so-called new order of tyranny" in order to show what might happen should the United States and the American people not support other nations in their fight against such tyranny.

Women's Suffrage

21. C
Difficulty: Medium

Category: Reading / Rhetoric

Strategic Advice: Keep in mind that the "stance" of an author refers to his or her perspective or attitude toward the topic.

Getting to the Answer: The passage is written by a secondary source, such as a scholar or a historian, who is looking back on the events that led to the adoption of the Nineteenth Amendment. It is not written by a primary source, such as a legislator or an advocate in the midst of the movement's events. For this reason, (C) is the correct answer. The author of the passage is most clearly a scholar evaluating not just the motivation of women's suffrage leaders but the key events and impact of the movement as a whole.

22. B
Difficulty: Hard

Category: Reading / Rhetoric

Strategic Advice: Avoid answers like A that refer to related issues not relevant to the passage's purpose and answers like D that go too far. The correct answer will identify a claim made explicitly in the quote.

Getting to the Answer: In the quote, the author notes that election laws following passage of the Nineteenth Amendment did not secure equal voting rights for all. From this statement, it is fairly clear that other groups of people still needed support for their voting rights. Answer (B) is correct.

23. D
Difficulty: Medium

Category: Reading / Command of Evidence

Strategic Advice: Reread the line quoted in the previous question and notice that it occurs in the passage after ratification of the Nineteenth Amendment. Therefore, the evidence you're looking for will refer to an event that came later.

Getting to the Answer: The author suggests that the Nineteenth Amendment did not win equal voting rights for all citizens but that it did serve as an important step on the way to free and fair elections. Choice (D) demonstrates that a later event expanded voting rights further, to citizens regardless not only of gender but also of race.

24. C
Difficulty: Easy

Category: Reading / Vocab-in-Context

Strategic Advice: Consider the events that are being described in the paragraph in which the word appears. This will help you choose the best answer.

Getting to the Answer: It's clear in this paragraph that the women's suffrage movement was gaining momentum at this time. Events and tactics excited those who supported the movement and attracted more supporters. Therefore, (C) reflects the correct meaning of "galvanized."

25. A
Difficulty: Hard

Category: Reading / Rhetoric

Strategic Advice: Carefully review the paragraph in which the line appears before choosing the best answer.

Getting to the Answer: Choice (A) demonstrates the connection between successfully changing one element (people's minds) in order to change the other (laws).

26. A
Difficulty: Hard

Category: Reading / Inference

Strategic Advice: Be wary of answers like D that go too far in asserting unsubstantiated causal relationships. The correct answer will reference an idea or a relationship that is supported by the content of the passage.

Getting to the Answer: Choice (A) expresses the idea implicit in the passage that the American government responds, sometimes slowly, to the changing needs and sentiments of the American people.

27. D
Difficulty: Hard

Category: Reading / Command of Evidence

Strategic Advice: Watch for answers like A and C that cite specific changes or examples that might seem to support the implicit meaning but do not go far enough. The correct answer will reflect the full relationship or idea described in the implicit meaning.

Getting to the Answer: The correct answer to the previous question states the idea implicit in the passage that the government responds and adapts to changes in U.S. society. This suggests a change that takes place over time. Choice (D) demonstrates the idea that both society and the government have changed over time as the civil rights movement of the late twentieth century overcame social and legal inequalities inherited from earlier in the nation's history.

28. C
Difficulty: Medium

Category: Reading / Detail

Strategic Advice: Be careful of answers that aren't backed by sufficient evidence in the graphic.

Getting to the Answer: The graphic shows proof that women's suffrage unfolded through a series of events over a long period of time. Choice (C) is the correct answer.

29. C
Difficulty: Medium

Category: Reading / Vocab-in-Context

Strategic Advice: Read the sentence in which the word appears. The correct answer should be interchangeable with the word.

Getting to the Answer: The passage states that "Posters . . . called into question the authenticity of a free country with unjust laws." Choice (C) is the correct answer, as "legitimacy" refers to something that is in accordance with established rules or principles.

30. B
Difficulty: Medium

Category: Reading / Inference

Strategic Advice: Be cautious about answers that state true events but that do not directly relate to the content of the question.

Getting to the Answer: Choice (B) is the correct answer. Wilson's framing of the conflict abroad as a fight for democracy and freedom helped women suffragists draw attention to the fact that the U.S. government was fighting for justice abroad while denying justice at home.

31. D
Difficulty: Medium

Category: Reading / Synthesis

Strategic Advice: A question like this is asking you to compare information provided in the graphic with information provided in the passage text. Consider each answer choice as you make your comparison.

Getting to the Answer: Choice (D) is the correct answer. Both the graphic and the passage indicate

that women's suffrage gained early victories in several states quite a few years before becoming law at the federal level through passage of the Nineteenth Amendment.

Paired Passages—Genomes

32. B
Difficulty: Medium

Category: Reading / Global

Strategic Advice: Look for the answer choice that describes an idea supported throughout the passage rather than a specific detail.

Getting to the Answer: Collectively, the details in the passage support the idea that the coffee market can be expanded and, as a result, the profits generated from coffee sales can be increased by applying information gained in sequencing the genome of coffee plants. Choice (B) is the correct answer.

33. B
Difficulty: Hard

Category: Reading / Rhetoric

Strategic Advice: Avoid answers that are not directly supported by evidence in the passage.

Getting to the Answer: Eliminate answers such as A and C, which are not supported by the main idea of the passage. In contrast, there is evidential support for (B). The author would most likely agree that studying other nonhuman primates could be beneficial to people.

34. C
Difficulty: Medium

Category: Reading / Inference

Strategic Advice: Watch out for answer choices that seem plausible but are not directly implied by the evidence in the passage.

Getting to the Answer: Choice (C) is the correct answer. In the last paragraph, the author discusses how research that is currently being conducted could impact the future of coffee production.

35. D

Difficulty: Medium

Category: Reading / Command of Evidence

Strategic Advice: Look back at the previous question. Find the lines from the passage that describe research that could increase the profitability of coffee for producers.

Getting to the Answer: Choice (D) is the correct answer. In the last paragraph, the author describes how current research could lead to a way to produce coffee plants without caffeine in a more cost-effective manner.

36. B

Difficulty: Hard

Category: Reading / Inference

Strategic Advice: Eliminate any answer choices that may sound plausible but take the information presented in the passage too far.

Getting to the Answer: The passage states that the research being conducted on the DNA of gibbons could provide scientists with a way to start figuring out how to prevent cancer and other human ailments. Choice (B) is the correct answer.

37. D

Difficulty: Medium

Category: Reading / Command of Evidence

Strategic Advice: Look at your answer for the previous question. Skim the passage to find the paragraph you used to select your answer.

Getting to the Answer: Choice (D) is the quote from the passage that directly supports the idea that more research would be needed before current findings could be applied to curing diseases in humans.

38. A

Difficulty: Medium

Category: Reading / Rhetoric

Strategic Advice: Remember that you're looking for a statement that expresses the purposes of both passages, not just one.

Getting to the Answer: Both passages discuss how sequencing the genome of a nonhuman organism can benefit people. Therefore, (A) is the correct answer.

39. B

Difficulty: Medium

Category: Reading / Vocab-in-Context

Strategic Advice: Be careful of answer choices that are synonyms for "compelled" but do not make sense in the context in which they're used in the passage.

Getting to the Answer: Choice (B) makes the most sense in context. The scientists felt driven to pursue genome sequencing of the coffee plant.

40. A

Difficulty: Easy

Category: Reading / Vocab-in-Context

Strategic Advice: Replace the word in the sentence with each answer choice and eliminate those that do not make sense in context.

Getting to the Answer: In the context, (A) makes the most sense. "Maintenance" most nearly means "preservation."

41. B
Difficulty: Hard

Category: Reading / Rhetoric

Strategic Advice: Be careful of answer choices that are not directly related to the phrase being considered.

Getting to the Answer: The author of Passage 1 is making a generalization about the coffee industry in order to introduce the main topic to the reader. The author uses the phrase a "pillar of the world economy" to show that the coffee industry plays a vital role in the world economy. Choice (B) is the correct answer.

42. D
Difficulty: Hard

Category: Reading / Synthesis

Strategic Advice: Be careful of answer choices that make inferences based on only one of the passages.

Getting to the Answer: Each passage describes a way that genome sequencing of an organism other than a human has benefited people. Therefore, (D) is the correct answer.

Biomimicry Passage

43. A
Difficulty: Medium

Category: Reading / Global

Strategic Advice: Look for the answer choice that describes an idea supported throughout the passage rather than a specific detail.

Getting to the Answer: The passage cites several examples of biomimicry, the study of how materials and systems found in nature can be replicated to benefit humans. Therefore, (A) is the best summary of the central idea of the passage.

44. B
Difficulty: Medium

Category: Reading / Command of Evidence

Strategic Advice: Think back to why you chose your answer to the previous question. This will help you pick the correct quote as evidence.

Getting to the Answer: Choice (B) is the correct answer because it provides evidence for the central idea that the author presents about the field of biomimicry.

45. A
Difficulty: Hard

Category: Reading / Rhetoric

Strategic Advice: Think about the main idea of the quote. Eliminate any answer choices that don't support this main idea.

Getting to the Answer: The quote explains why architects turn to biomimicry for solutions in their work. Choice (A) is the correct answer.

46. B
Difficulty: Medium

Category: Reading / Inference

Strategic Advice: Reread the paragraph that the question is asking about. Look for specific details about the abalone shrimp shell and soft chalk.

Getting to the Answer: The passage clearly states that the abalone shrimp shell is harder than soft chalk because of the way the basic material composing each is arranged, so (B) is the correct answer.

47. D
Difficulty: Medium

Category: Reading / Rhetoric

Strategic Advice: In order to understand why an author includes a quote from another person, examine the surrounding sentences. This often makes clear the author's reason for including the quotation.

Getting to the Answer: The author includes the quote from Pawlyn to support and strengthen his or her own view that energy efficiency "has never been more important." Therefore, (D) is the correct answer.

48. D
Difficulty: Easy

Category: Reading / Vocab-in-Context

Strategic Advice: Replace the word in question with each of the answer choices. This will help you eliminate the ones that don't make sense in the context.

Getting to the Answer: Choice (D), "theories," is the only answer choice that makes sense in this context.

49. A
Difficulty: Medium

Category: Reading / Inference

Strategic Advice: Keep in mind that you're being asked to make an inference, a logical guess based on information in the passage. Therefore, the correct answer is not stated in a passage.

Getting to the Answer: The variety of examples of biomimicry mentioned in the passage make it reasonable to infer that more scientists will utilize solutions developed through biomimicry in the future. Choice (A) is the correct answer.

50. C
Difficulty: Medium

Category: Reading / Command of Evidence

Strategic Advice: Reread each quotation in the context of the passage. Consider which one is the best evidence to support the inference made in the previous question.

Getting to the Answer: The examples cited in (C) provide strong evidence for the inference that more scientists will probably make use of biomimicry in years to come.

51. D
Difficulty: Medium

Category: Reading / Vocab-in-Context

Strategic Advice: Eliminate answer choices that are synonyms for the word in question but do not work in the context of the sentence.

Getting to the Answer: Because biomimicry is such an innovative approach, it makes sense that the meaning of "radical" in this context is closest to (D), "revolutionary."

52. C
Difficulty: Hard

Category: Reading / Synthesis

Strategic Advice: Remember that a graphic might not refer to something explicitly stated in the passage. Instead, it often provides a visual example of how an important concept discussed in the passage works.

Getting to the Answer: The graphic and its caption help illustrate an example of biomimicry not mentioned in the passage: that of a solar power plant designed to mimic the arrangement of petals in a sunflower. This directs more energy toward the power plant's central tower and improves the efficiency of the power plant. Choice (C) is the correct answer.

WRITING AND LANGUAGE TEST

The Age of the Librarian

1. C
Difficulty: Easy

Category: Writing & Language / Shifts in Construction

Strategic Advice: Examine the verb tense in the rest of the sentence. This will help you find the correct answer.

Getting to the Answer: As written, the sentence switches verb tense midsentence. Other verbs in the sentence, "worked" and "was," indicate that the events happened in the past. Choice (C) is the correct choice because it correctly uses the past tense of the target verb.

2. D
Difficulty: Medium

Category: Writing & Language / Punctuation

Strategic Advice: Pay attention to the quotation marks. Make sure a complete sentence is properly punctuated within the quotation marks.

Getting to the Answer: Reading through the sentence and the answer choices shows that two issues might need correcting. The sentence inside the quotation marks is a complete sentence. The correct answer needs to punctuate that sentence before closing the quote. Additionally, "however" is being used as a connector or transition word and needs to be followed by a comma after beginning the new sentence. Choice (D) appropriately uses a period prior to the end quotes and correctly inserts a comma after the transition "However."

3. B
Difficulty: Medium

Category: Writing & Language / Effective Language Use

Strategic Advice: Watch out for choices that distort the tone of the passage.

Getting to the Answer: The passage suggests that people expected or anticipated that Harris would become a librarian. Evidence for this idea is found in the statement that she was "constantly told" that she "should be studying to be a librarian." Harris was certainly aware that people anticipated this course of study for her, but the presence of the phrase "Little did she realize" tells you that she didn't expect to become one. The correct choice is (B), "imminent," meaning that becoming a librarian was about to occur despite her own expectations.

4. C
Difficulty: Hard

Category: Writing & Language / Effective Language Use

Strategic Advice: Read the sentence carefully for context clues. Also, think about the tone of what is being described. This will help you choose the best answer.

Getting to the Answer: Given the phrasing of the sentence, the answer must be close in meaning to "excited," which is used earlier in the sentence. Therefore, (C) is the correct answer.

5. A
Difficulty: Medium

Category: Writing & Language / Punctuation

Strategic Advice: Determine whether a clause is independent or dependent to decide between a comma and a semicolon.

Getting to the Answer: Choice (A) is the correct answer. The sentence is correctly punctuated as written because it uses a comma at the end of the introductory clause.

6. C
Difficulty: Medium

Category: Writing & Language / Sentence Formation

Strategic Advice: Read the sentence carefully. The sentence sounds clunky and awkward. Look for an answer choice that makes the sentence clear and easy to understand. Notice that the word "asking" is part of a participial phrase that modifies "Miguel."

Getting to the Answer: A participial phrase should be placed as close as possible to the noun it modifies. When a participial phrase begins a sentence, it should be set off with a comma.

Choice (C) is correct. The placement of commas and modifiers makes the content easy to understand, and the sentence is free of grammatical or punctuation errors.

7. B
Difficulty: Medium

Category: Writing & Language / Development

Strategic Advice: Read the entire paragraph carefully and predict the main idea. Then look for a close match with your prediction.

Getting to the Answer: The paragraph discusses how the role of librarian has changed due to an increased use of technology. Choice (B) is the correct answer, as it explicitly addresses the changing role of the librarian due to technology.

8. D
Difficulty: Medium

Category: Writing & Language / Sentence Formation

Strategic Advice: Read the sentence and note the series of examples. A series should have parallel structure.

Getting to the Answer: The sentence is not correct as written. The items in the series switch forms from participial phrases beginning with "enabling" and "offering" to "they house." All of the items need to fit the same pattern or form. Choice (D) is correct because it appropriately begins each item in the series with a participle.

9. C
Difficulty: Hard

Category: Writing & Language / Development

Strategic Advice: Don't be fooled by answer choices that are true statements but do not directly support the main idea of the paragraph.

Getting to the Answer: The paragraph concerns how the role of the librarian has changed due to an increased use of technology. The correct answer needs to support the idea that librarians work with technology in new ways. Choice (C) works best. It offers a specific example of how teachers look to the librarian to be a "media mentor" and illustrates this new role for school librarians.

10. C
Difficulty: Easy

Category: Writing & Language / Usage

Strategic Advice: Read the sentence prior to the pronoun and determine whom the pronoun is referencing. Pronouns should not be ambiguous, and they must match the verb in number.

Getting to the Answer: The sentence is ambiguous as written. "She" would presumably refer back to the "young student," but it seems unlikely that the student would be laughing and thinking about the collections in the library after asking the librarian a question. Choice (C) is the best choice. It clearly indicates the subject of the sentence (Harris) and avoids ambiguity.

11. A
Difficulty: Medium

Category: Writing & Language / Usage

Strategic Advice: Figure out whom the pronoun refers to and make sure it matches the antecedent in number. Watch out for confusing contractions and possessives.

Getting to the Answer: The pronoun in the sentence needs to indicate who will have the ideas. Harris is talking to a single student, so you will need a singular possessive pronoun.

Choice (A) is correct. As it is, the sentence correctly uses a singular possessive pronoun.

Unforeseen Consequences: The Dark Side of the Industrial Revolution

12. B
Difficulty: Medium

Category: Writing & Language / Sentence Formation

Strategic Advice: Be careful of answers that sound correct when they stand alone but do not conform to the structure of the sentence as a whole.

Getting to the Answer: The existing text is incorrect, as it does not maintain parallel structure. Choice (B) is the correct answer, as it maintains the parallel structure of preposition ("into") + noun ("the role").

13. B
Difficulty: Easy

Category: Writing & Language / Punctuation

Strategic Advice: Eliminate answers that confuse the usage of commas and semicolons.

Getting to the Answer: Choice (B) is correct. Without the comma, the following clause modifies "urban areas" when it should modify the entire preceding clause.

14. B
Difficulty: Medium

Category: Writing & Language / Effective Language Use

Strategic Advice: Avoid choices that are redundant and imprecise. The correct answer will use the clearest, most concise terminology to communicate the idea.

Getting to the Answer: Choice (B) is correct. It is the most concise—and clearest—word choice. The other choices use more words than necessary to convey meaning.

15. A
Difficulty: Medium

Category: Writing & Language / Organization

Strategic Advice: The first sentence should function as a transition between ideas in the previous paragraph and ideas in the current paragraph.

Getting to the Answer: Choice (A) makes sense. This choice connects ideas from the previous paragraph with the content of paragraph 3. The sentences that follow provide details to support that introductory idea.

16. A
Difficulty: Hard

Category: Writing & Language / Development

Strategic Advice: Eliminate answers like B that fail to directly support the cited sentence.

Getting to the Answer: The underlined sentence references "unprecedented amounts of human-made carbon dioxide into the air." This suggests an increase in the amount of carbon dioxide in the atmosphere over time. Therefore, (A) is the correct answer.

17. C
Difficulty: Medium

Category: Writing & Language / Effective Language Use

Strategic Advice: Choose the answer that presents the correct relationship between ideas.

Getting to the Answer: Choice (C) is correct. It shows the causal relationship without adding verbiage.

18. A
Difficulty: Easy

Category: Writing & Language / Effective Language Use

Strategic Advice: Plug in the answer choices and select the one that reflects a specific meaning relevant to the sentence.

Getting to the Answer: The paragraph focuses on the negative effects of industrialization and waste production. Therefore, (A) is the correct answer.

19. B
Difficulty: Hard

Category: Writing & Language / Development

Strategic Advice: Be careful of choices that relate to the underlined portion of the text without showing clearly how the underlined portion supports the full implication of the preceding sentence.

Getting to the Answer: The paragraph explains that industrialization resulted in the destruction of resources. The correct answer, (B), serves as clear evidence of the "process of destruction and reduced resources."

20. C
Difficulty: Medium

Category: Writing & Language / Effective Language Use

Strategic Advice: Be careful of answers that make sense but do not fully support the meaning of the content. The correct answer will not only flow logically but will also reflect the precise purpose and meaning of the larger sentence and paragraph.

Getting to the Answer: Choice (C) is the correct answer. "Substandard" communicates clearly that the working conditions were the cause of the health problems.

21. D
Difficulty: Medium

Category: Writing & Language / Sentence Formation

Strategic Advice: Eliminate choices that result in sentence fragments or fragmented clauses. The correct answer will maintain appropriate syntax without misusing punctuation.

Getting to the Answer: Choice (D) is correct. It sets off the dependent clause without using incorrect punctuation to signal a hard break before an independent clause or second complete sentence.

22. D
Difficulty: Hard

Category: Writing & Language / Development

Strategic Advice: Avoid answers that draw on similar ideas but combine those ideas in a way that communicates a proposition not supported by the essay as a whole. The correct answer will make sense within the larger context of the essay.

Getting to the Answer: The central idea of the entire essay is that industrialization and progress came at a cost that made the promise of a bright future difficult to fulfill. Choice (D) is the correct answer.

Remembering Freud

23. C
Difficulty: Hard

Category: Writing & Language / Effective Language Use

Strategic Advice: Consider the fact that there may be a choice that helps make the meaning of the sentence very precise.

Getting to the Answer: Choice (C) most accurately indicates that Freud led a whole movement.

24. B
Difficulty: Medium

Category: Writing & Language / Punctuation

Strategic Advice: Plug in each answer choice and select the one that seems most correct.

Getting to the Answer: Choice (B) makes it clear to the reader that this is extra information modifying the word "career."

25. D
Difficulty: Medium

Category: Writing & Language / Sentence Formation

Strategic Advice: Remember that in a list, all things listed should be presented with the same grammatical structure.

Getting to the Answer: "Id," "ego," and "Freudian slip" are all nouns. Choice (D) is the correct answer because it uses a parallel structure for all three nouns.

26. B
Difficulty: Hard

Category: Writing & Language / Development

Strategic Advice: Notice that the underlined sentence is the first sentence in the paragraph. Think about which choice would make the best topic sentence, given the content of the rest of the paragraph.

Getting to the Answer: Choice (B) correctly makes the free-speaking technique the focus of the paragraph's topic sentence, while suggesting that the technique was radical enough to earn Freud his title.

27. B
Difficulty: Medium

Category: Writing & Language / Effective Language Use

Strategic Advice: Eliminate any choices that don't seem as precise as others.

Getting to the Answer: Choice (B) is correct. The word "recesses" is more precise; it connotes smaller parts of the brain and a sense of being hidden.

28. C
Difficulty: Easy

Category: Writing & Language / Punctuation

Strategic Advice: Try reading the sentence in question aloud. This often helps you get a good sense of whether or not a comma is needed.

Getting to the Answer: Choice (C) would fit here. The sentence eliminates the unneeded comma and is a correct sentence.

29. B
Difficulty: Hard

Category: Writing & Language / Sentence Formation

Strategic Advice: Remember that a modifier should be adjacent to the noun it is modifying and set off by punctuation.

Getting to the Answer: Choice (B) is correct. The modifier "like neurosis or other psychological trauma" should come directly after "conditions."

30. C
Difficulty: Hard

Category: Writing & Language / Development

Strategic Advice: Consider how this sentence relates to the one before it and the one that follows it. Does it offer strong support of the connecting ideas?

Getting to the Answer: This section discussed the development and lasting influence of Freud's ideas. The best supporting sentence will provide details connecting these concepts. Choice (C) is correct. It emphasizes that Freud developed new ideas that have had a lasting influence on psychological practices.

31. B
Difficulty: Medium

Category: Writing & Language / Sentence Formation

Strategic Advice: Notice that you are dealing with a run-on sentence. Identify the point in the run-on where it appears two sentences have been fused together.

Getting to the Answer: Choice (B) is correct. This choice splits the run-on sentence into two separate, grammatically correct sentences.

32. D
Difficulty: Easy

Category: Writing & Language / Sentence Formation

Strategic Advice: Eliminate answer choices that are not complete sentences or do not maintain the correct verb tense.

Getting to the Answer: Choice (D) correctly changes the phrase "Freud's finding of a method" to "Freud

found a method," making the sentence complete. It also corrects the verb tense.

33. A
Difficulty: Hard

Category: Writing & Language / Sentence Formation

Strategic Advice: Recall that when a dependent clause precedes an independent clause, it should be set off with a comma.

Getting to the Answer: Choice (A) is the best choice. Although lengthy, the dependent clause in the sentence ("So as long as occasions arise . . . ") is correctly combined with its independent clause ("Sigmund Freud will be remembered . . . ") by use of a comma.

Success in Montreal

34. B
Difficulty: Easy

Category: Writing & Language / Sentence Formation

Strategic Advice: Always check whether two or more verbs that serve the same function have a parallel structure.

Getting to the Answer: Choice (B) is correct. "To prevent" is in the infinitive form like the first verb in the sentence, "to reverse."

35. A
Difficulty: Hard

Category: Writing & Language / Effective Language Use

Strategic Advice: Look for the choice that most concisely and correctly joins the two sentences.

Getting to the Answer: Choice (A) is the best fit. This option joins the sentences concisely and correctly.

36. C
Difficulty: Medium

Category: Writing & Language / Effective Language Use

Strategic Advice: Remember that the best answer is the most concise and effective way of stating the information while ensuring that the information is complete.

Getting to the Answer: Choice (C) works best here. It uses the fewest necessary words to convey the complete information.

37. C
Difficulty: Medium

Category: Writing & Language / Sentence Formation

Strategic Advice: Eliminate any choices that use transition words inappropriately.

Getting to the Answer: Two complete thoughts should be separated into two different sentences. Therefore, (C) is the best choice.

38. B
Difficulty: Hard

Category: Writing & Language / Quantitative

Strategic Advice: Examine the graphic for details that suggest which answer is correct.

Getting to the Answer: Choice (B) accurately reflects the information in the graphic. Beginning in the 1990s, the size of the ozone hole began to level off.

39. C
Difficulty: Medium

Category: Writing & Language / Effective Language Use

Strategic Advice: Check each word to see how it fits with the context of the sentence.

Getting to the Answer: While all of the words have similar meanings, only one fits the context of the paragraph. Choice (C), "measured," has a connotation that corresponds to "gauge" in the following sentence.

40. B
Difficulty: Easy

Category: Writing & Language / Usage

Strategic Advice: Remember that the possessive form must agree with its antecedent.

Getting to the Answer: The correct answer will reflect the gender and number of its antecedent; in this case, the word "treaty." Therefore, (B) is correct.

41. A
Difficulty: Hard

Category: Writing & Language / Development

Strategic Advice: To find the central idea of a paragraph, identify important details and then summarize them in a sentence or two. Then find the choice that is the closest to your summary.

Getting to the Answer: Choice (A) most clearly states the paragraph's central idea.

42. D
Difficulty: Medium

Category: Writing & Language / Development

Strategic Advice: To find the correct answer, first determine the central idea of the paragraph.

Getting to the Answer: Choice (D) is the least essential sentence in the paragraph, so it is the correct answer.

43. D
Difficulty: Medium

Category: Writing & Language / Effective Language Use

Strategic Advice: Context clues tell which word is appropriate in the sentence. Check to see which word fits best in the sentence.

Getting to the Answer: The word "reverse," (D), fits with the context of the sentence and connotes a more precise action than does "change."

44. C
Difficulty: Hard

Category: Writing & Language / Organization

Strategic Advice: Examine the entire paragraph. Decide whether the sentence provides more information about a topic mentioned in one of the other sentences.

Getting to the Answer: This sentence provides more information related to sentence 1, "The Montreal Protocol is a living document"; it describes how the document is "living." Choice (C) is the correct answer.

ESSAY TEST RUBRIC

The Essay Demonstrates . . .

4—Advanced	• **(Reading)** A strong ability to comprehend the source text, including its central ideas and important details and how they interrelate; and effectively use evidence (quotations, paraphrases, or both) from the source text.
	• **(Analysis)** A strong ability to evaluate the author's use of evidence, reasoning, and/or stylistic and persuasive elements, and/or other features of the student's own choosing; make good use of relevant, sufficient, and strategically chosen support for the claims or points made in the student's essay; and focus consistently on features of the source text that are most relevant to addressing the task.
	• **(Writing)** A strong ability to provide a precise central claim; create an effective organization that includes an introduction and conclusion, as well as a clear progression of ideas; successfully employ a variety of sentence structures; use precise word choice; maintain a formal style and objective tone; and show command of the conventions of standard written English so that the essay is free of errors.
3—Proficient	• **(Reading)** Satisfactory ability to comprehend the source text, including its central ideas and important details and how they interrelate; and use evidence (quotations, paraphrases, or both) from the source text.
	• **(Analysis)** Satisfactory ability to evaluate the author's use of evidence, reasoning, and/or stylistic and persuasive elements, and/or other features of the student's own choosing; make use of relevant and sufficient support for the claims or points made in the student's essay; and focus primarily on features of the source text that are most relevant to addressing the task.
	• **(Writing)** Satisfactory ability to provide a central claim; create an organization that includes an introduction and conclusion, as well as a clear progression of ideas; employ a variety of sentence structures; use precise word choice; maintain an appropriate formal style and objective tone; and show control of the conventions of standard written English so that the essay is free of significant errors.
2—Partial	• **(Reading)** Limited ability to comprehend the source text, including its central ideas and important details and how they interrelate; and use evidence (quotations, paraphrases, or both) from the source text.
	• **(Analysis)** Limited ability to evaluate the author's use of evidence, reasoning, and/or stylistic and persuasive elements, and/or other features of the student's own choosing; make use of support for the claims or points made in the student's essay; and focus on relevant features of the source text.
	• **(Writing)** Limited ability to provide a central claim; create an effective organization for ideas; employ a variety of sentence structures; use precise word choice; maintain an appropriate style and tone; or show control of the conventions of standard written English, resulting in certain errors that detract from the quality of the writing.

1—Inadequate	• **(Reading)** Little or no ability to comprehend the source text or use evidence from the source text. • **(Analysis)** Little or no ability to evaluate the author's use of evidence, reasoning, and/or stylistic and persuasive elements; choose support for claims or points; or focus on relevant features of the source text. • **(Writing)** Little or no ability to provide a central claim, organization, or progression of ideas; employ a variety of sentence structures; use precise word choice; maintain an appropriate style and tone; or show control of the conventions of standard written English, resulting in numerous errors that undermine the quality of the writing.

SAMPLE ESSAY RESPONSE #1 (ADVANCED SCORE)

As anyone knows who has had to help their family move house, find a textbook in a cluttered room, or even just clean a crowded apartment, possessions can have a huge amount of power over people. Far from being simply objects that we enjoy or that bring us pleasure, it can sometimes feel that our possessions oppress us. This is the point Morris eloquently makes in her essay "The Tyranny of Things." By using anecdotes, examples, reasoning, and powerful imagery, Morris argues that the very things we cherish are nearly crushing the life out of us.

The author begins by relating an anecdote about two teenagers becoming fast friends over their love of things. It is a touching moment, one to which readers can easily relate; even Morris herself says that we all probably go through this phase. This helps establish her credibility with readers, because her examples make sense to them. Gradually, however, Morris makes it clear that this touching moment has a sinister side—the love of things will only result in resentment.

Morris reasons that while it's natural to go through a phase of wanting objects, it is unhealthy to remain in this state. "Many people never pass out of this phase," she writes ominously. "They never see a flower without wanting to pick it . . . they bring home all their alpenstocks." It begins to sound obsessive, this need to control things. Morris goes on to develop her argument by suggesting that possessions are metaphorically suffocating us. She makes the idea of too many possessions sound repulsive by describing them as "an undigested mass of things." The things almost take on a kind of life force, according to Morris: "they possess us." They "have destroyed" our empty spaces and we feel "stifled."

Another way Morris supports her argument is by giving examples of the unnecessary "tokens" associated with social occasions. She describes how at events, luncheons, and parties, gifts are given and received. She then uses powerful negative imagery to describe the effects of these gifts, comparing the recipient to a "ship encrusted with barnacles" that needs to be "scraped bare again." This language suggests that the gifts are burdensome and even harmful.

By contrast, the imagery Morris uses to describe a simple life filled with fewer things is imagery of ease and relaxation. "We breathe more freely in the clear space that we have made for ourselves," she writes. It is not just that we have literally regained control from our possessions and are now acting rather than being acted upon; it is that we are physically more at ease.

In her conclusion, Morris longs for a day when we can live more simply, with fewer possessions. She describes a "house by the sea" that was simple and empty; it did not "demand care" or "claim attention" or otherwise act upon her. Her wish is that "we could but free ourselves" from the tyranny of things that she feels is draining us of our freedom. And at this point, it is likely the reader's wish, too.

SAMPLE ESSAY RESPONSE #2 (PROFICIENT SCORE)

Although as people we like to think of ourselves as owners of things, in fact it can sometimes feel like the things we own end up owning us. At least this is what Morris argues in her essay "The Tyranny of Things." Through her use of evidence, reasoning, and word choice, she makes a strong argument that we should own fewer things if we ever want to be truly happy.

Morris tells a story about two teenage girls who instantly know they will be friends because they both like things. They are not happy just to be. They have to own things. It's like their own experiences aren't enough for them. But Morris says that this is bad for people, because they will end up feeling like their possessions own them.

Morris's reasoning is that we can basically get control back over our own lives if we stop needing things so much. If we have too many things, "they possess us." So we have to get rid of things, and then we can feel better. At least these days we aren't buried with our things anymore, like they were in the olden days.

The word choices in the essay are interesting. She talks about the way things become a problem for us: "our books are a burden to us, our pictures have destroyed every restful wall-space, our china is a care." By using a lot of repetition, it shows how powerful things are.

Morris's essay encourages people to free themselves from their things. If they do so, they will be happier. Through her personal anecdotes, reasoning, and repetitive word choices, she makes her essay very powerful.